Welcome to "Nature's Serenity: Stress-Relieving Coloring Book for Adults." In this book, you will find an array of beautifully detailed designs inspired by the tranquility and beauty of nature. Each page is crafted to provide you with a peaceful and relaxing coloring experience, allowing you to immerse yourself in the calming effects of nature's wonders.

Whether you are a seasoned coloring enthusiast or new to this creative outlet, "Nature's Serenity" is designed to help you unwind, reduce stress, and reconnect with the soothing rhythm of the natural world. As you color each intricate illustration, let your mind wander through serene landscapes, vibrant floral patterns, and the quiet charm of various natural settings.

Take a deep breath, pick up your favorite coloring tools, and let the stress of the day melt away as you bring these pages to life. Welcome to a journey of relaxation and artistic expression.

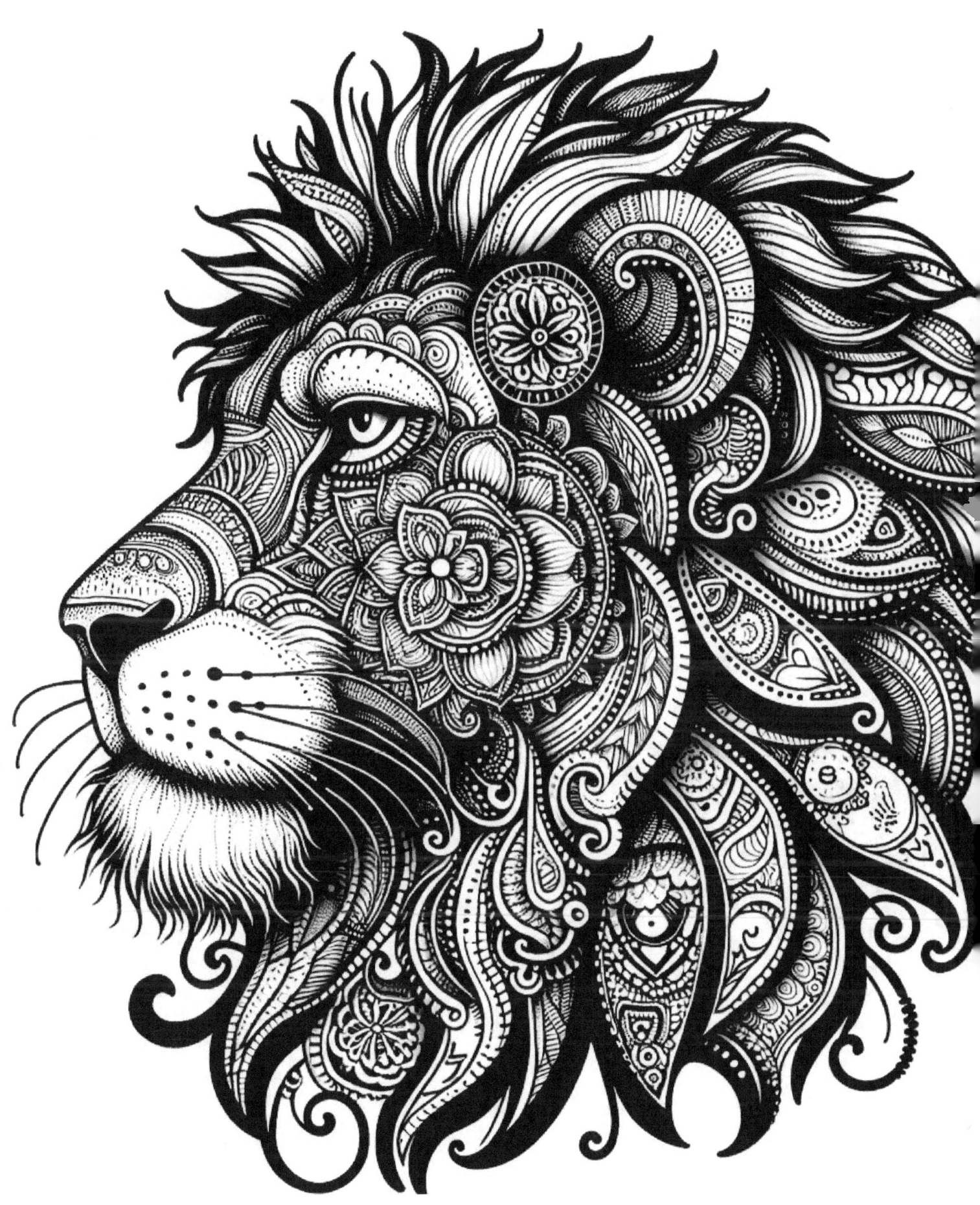

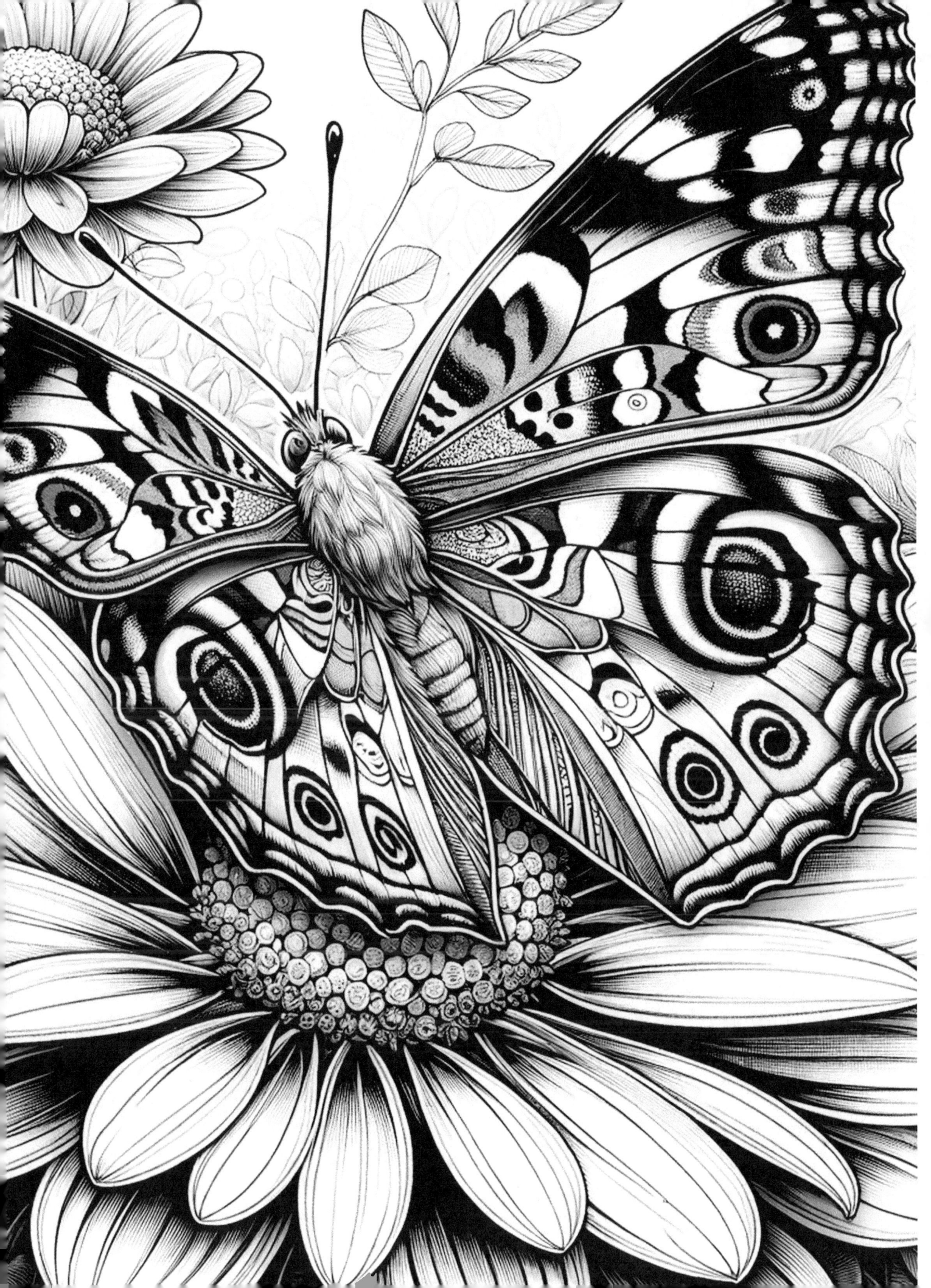

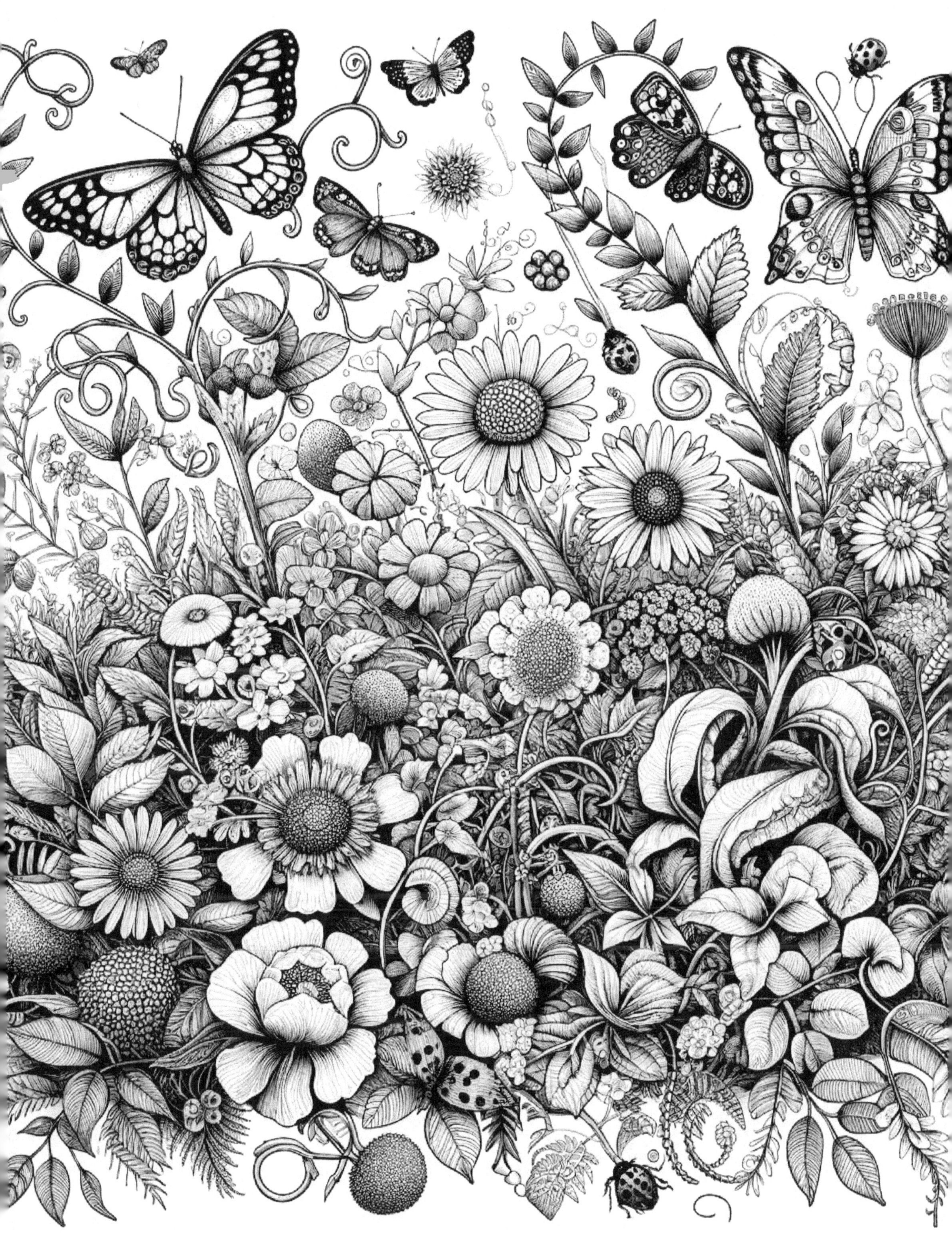

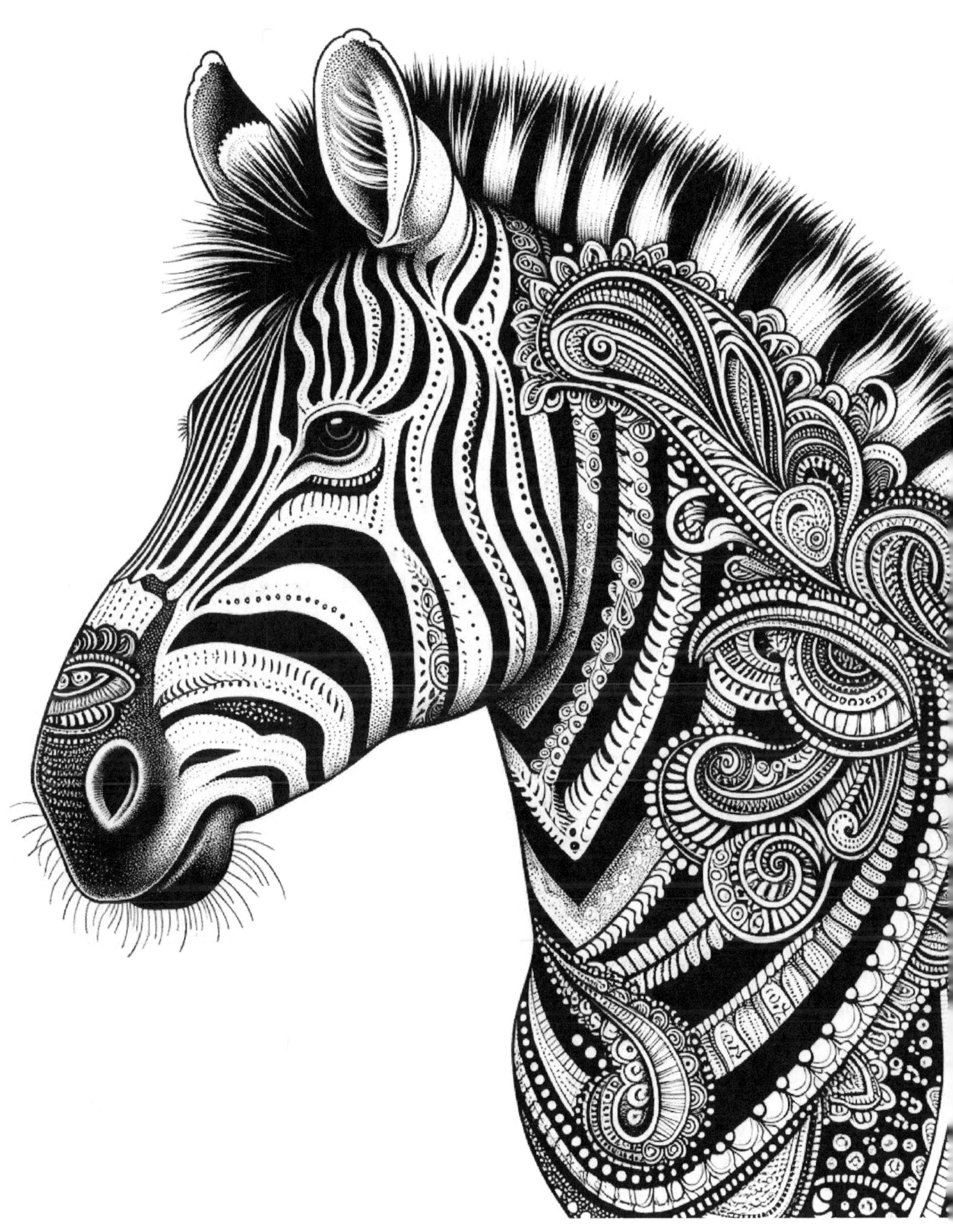

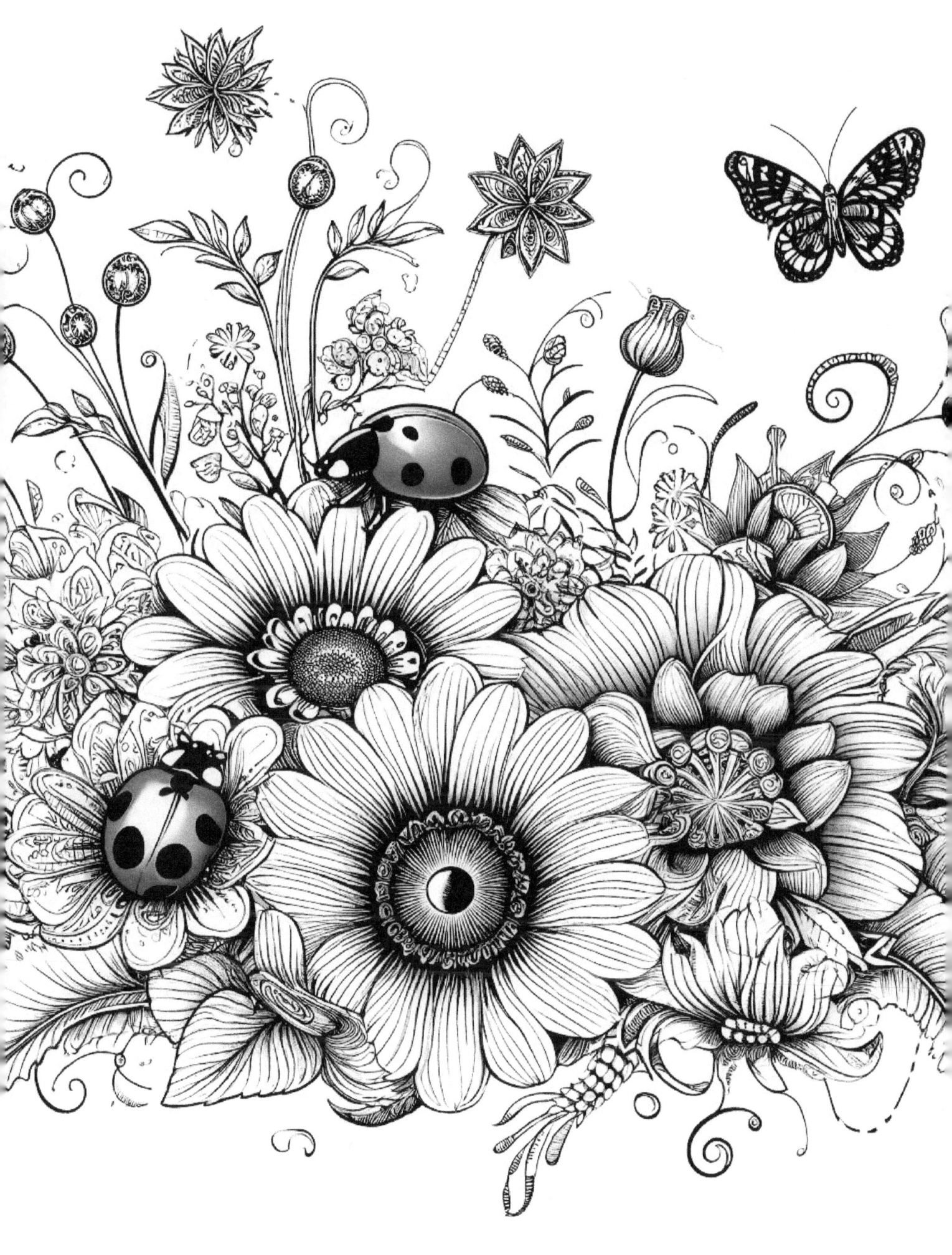

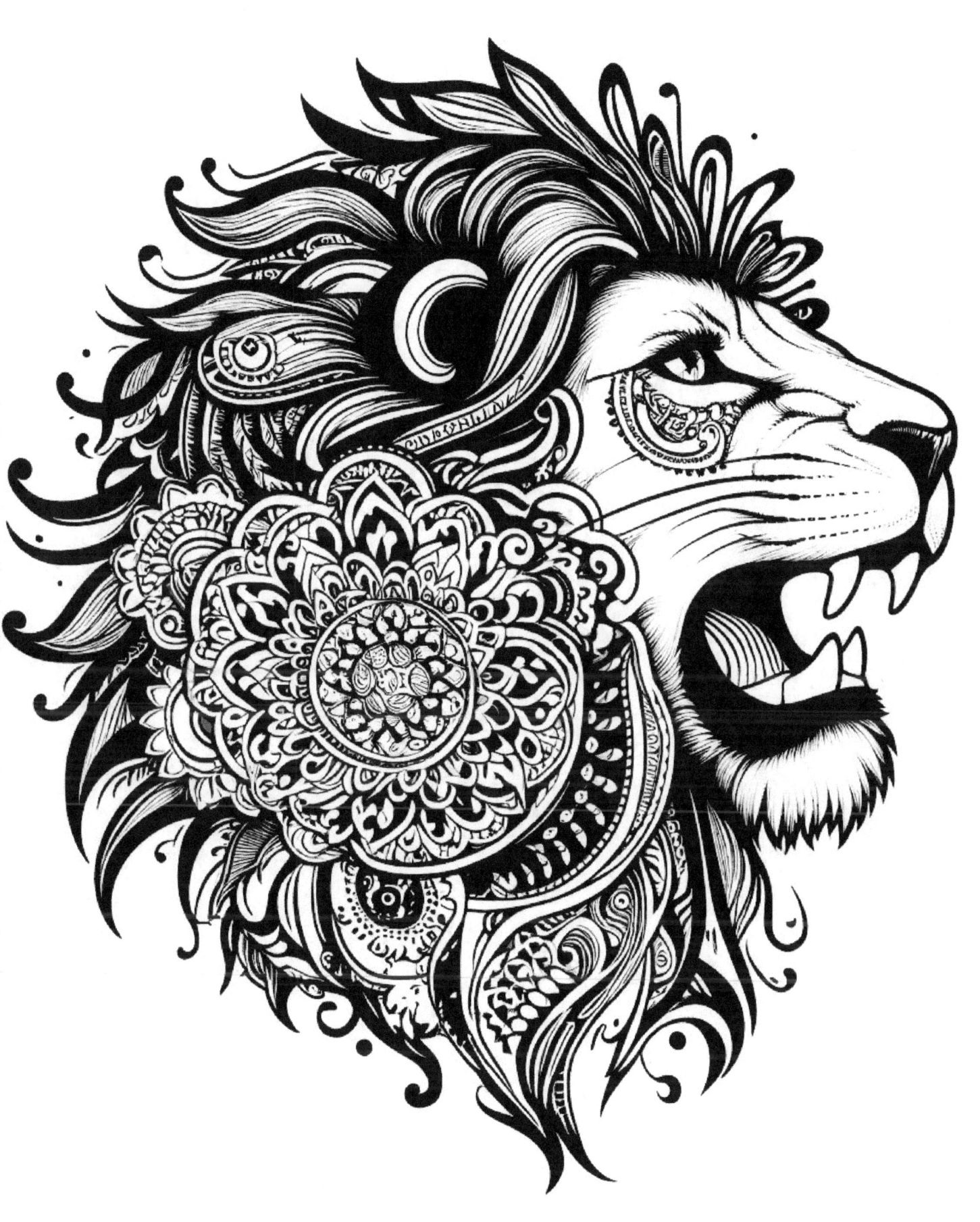

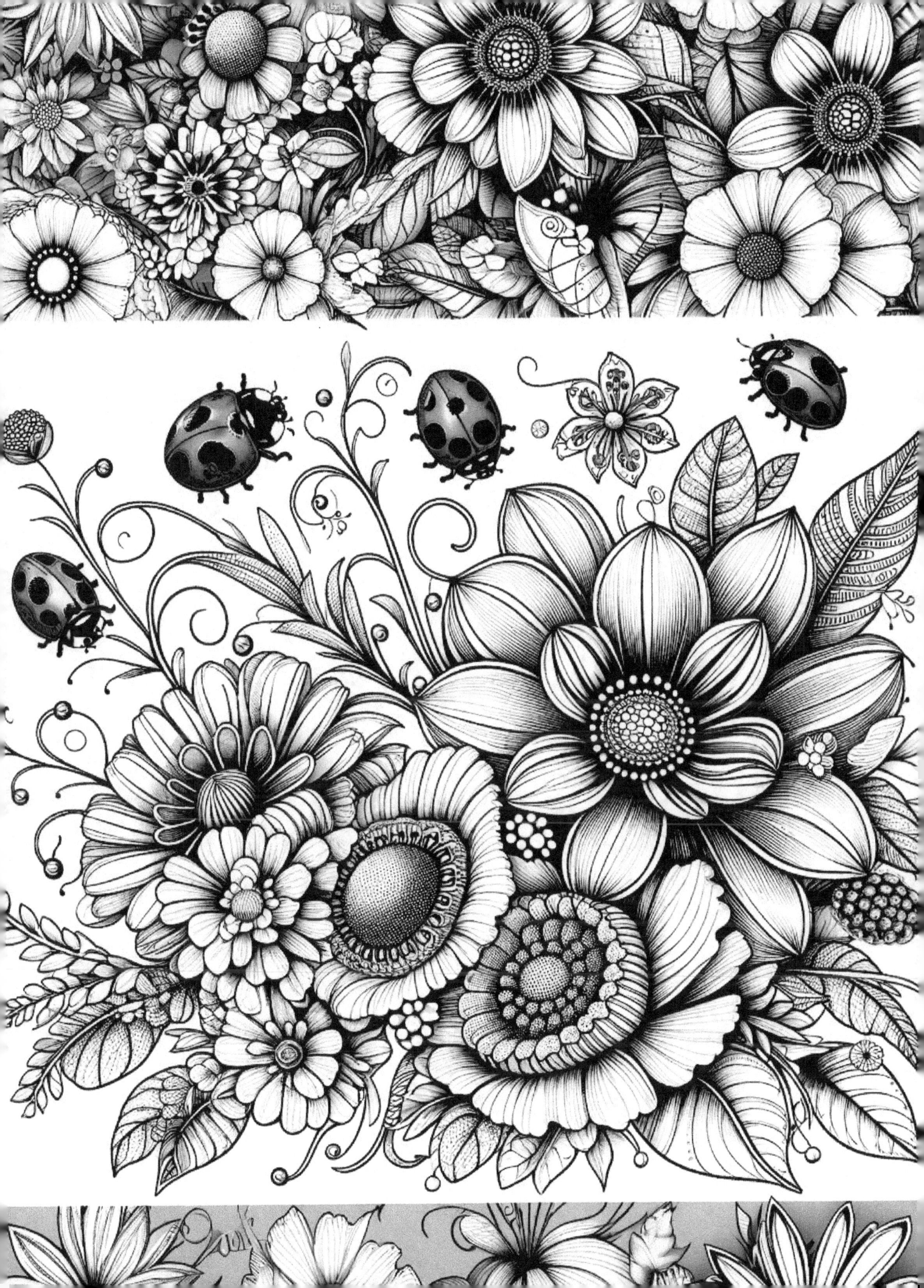

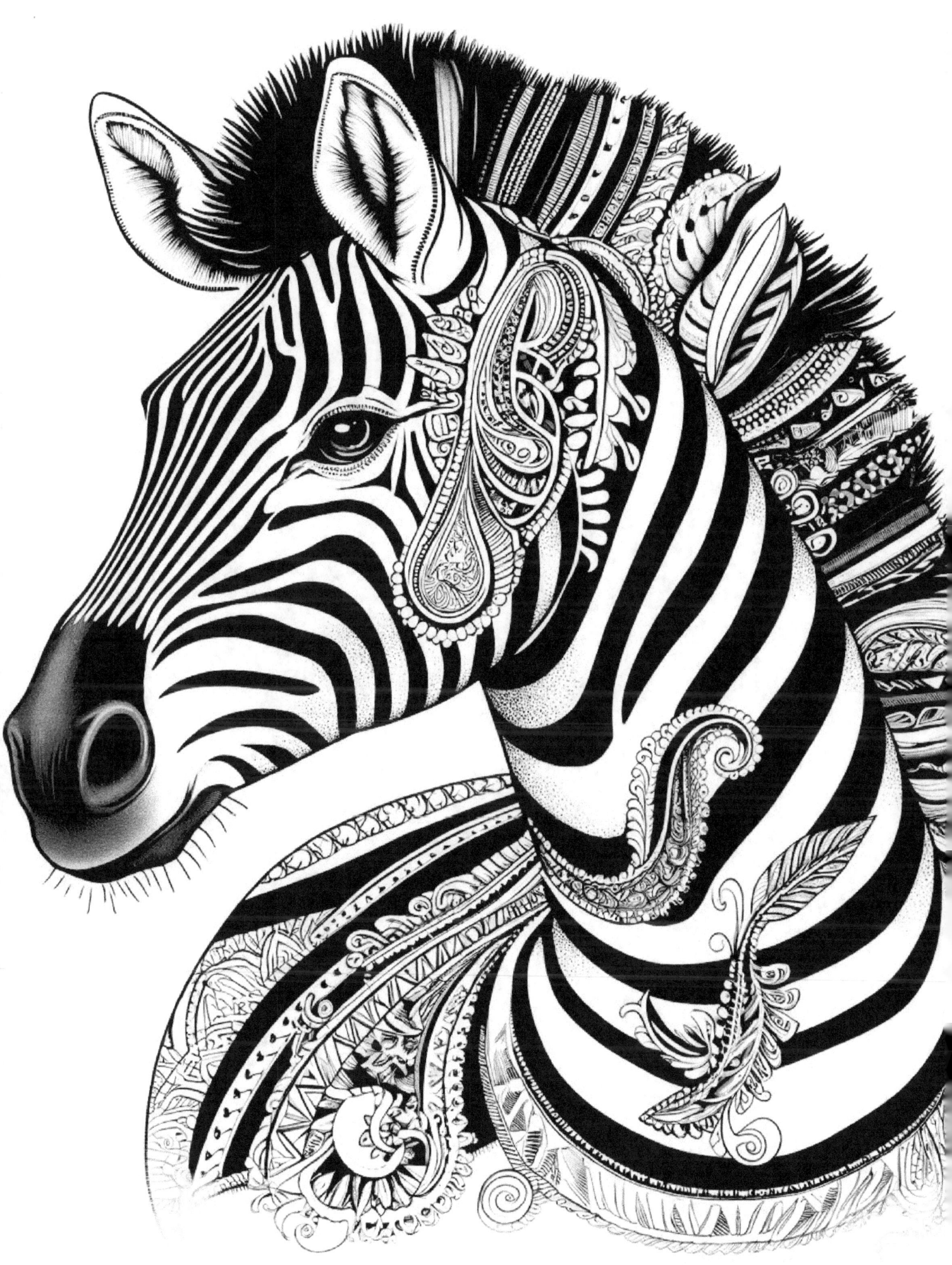

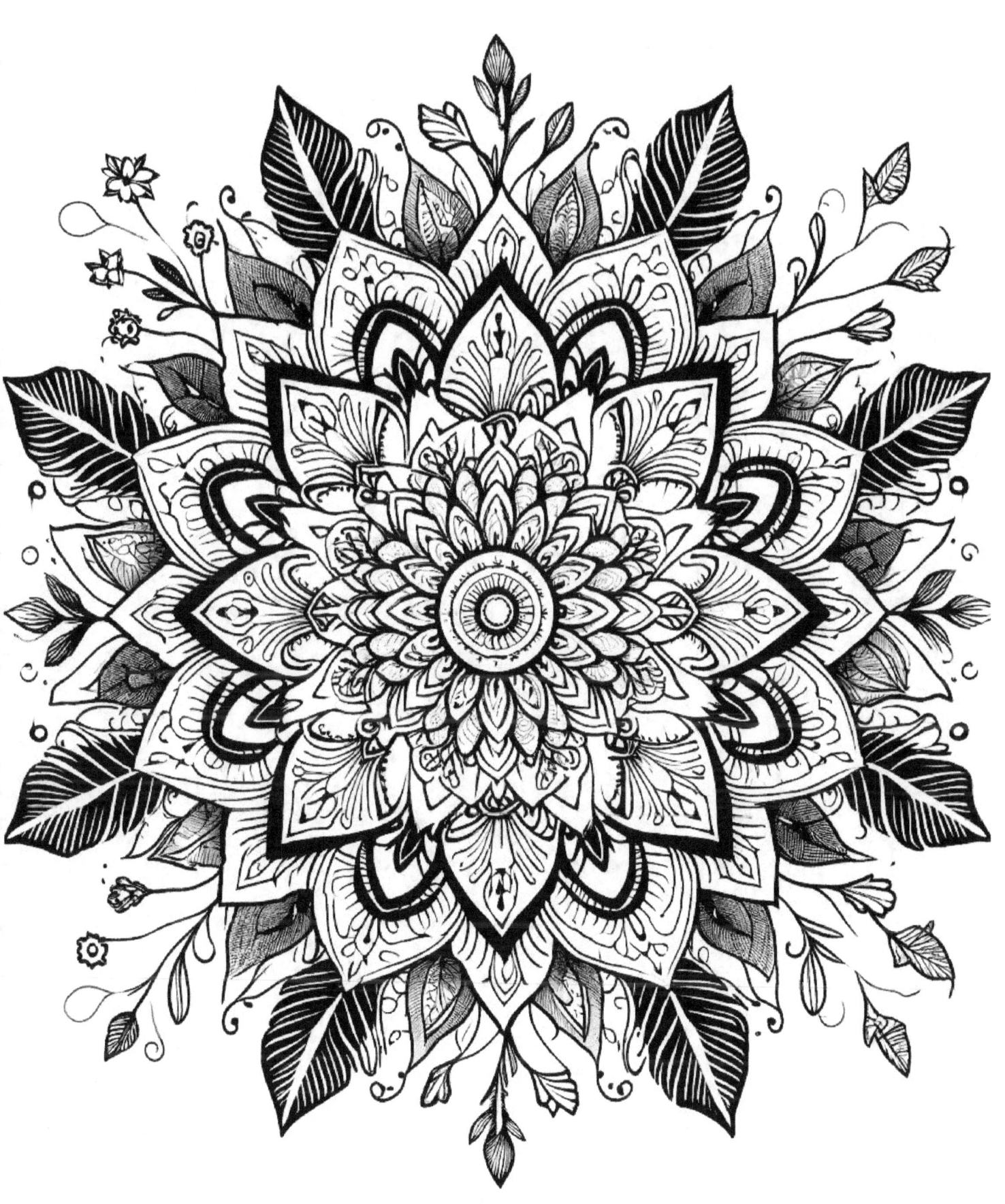

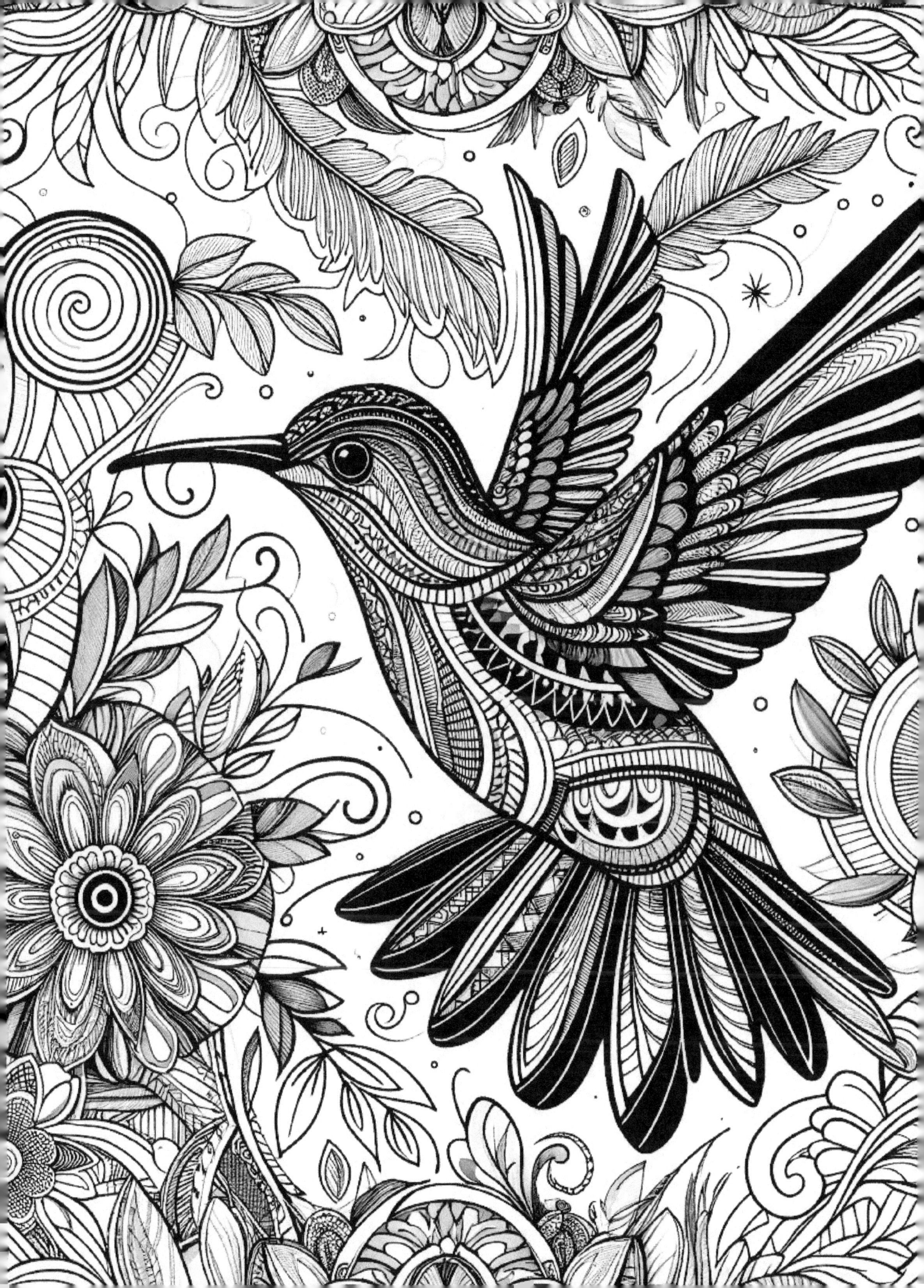

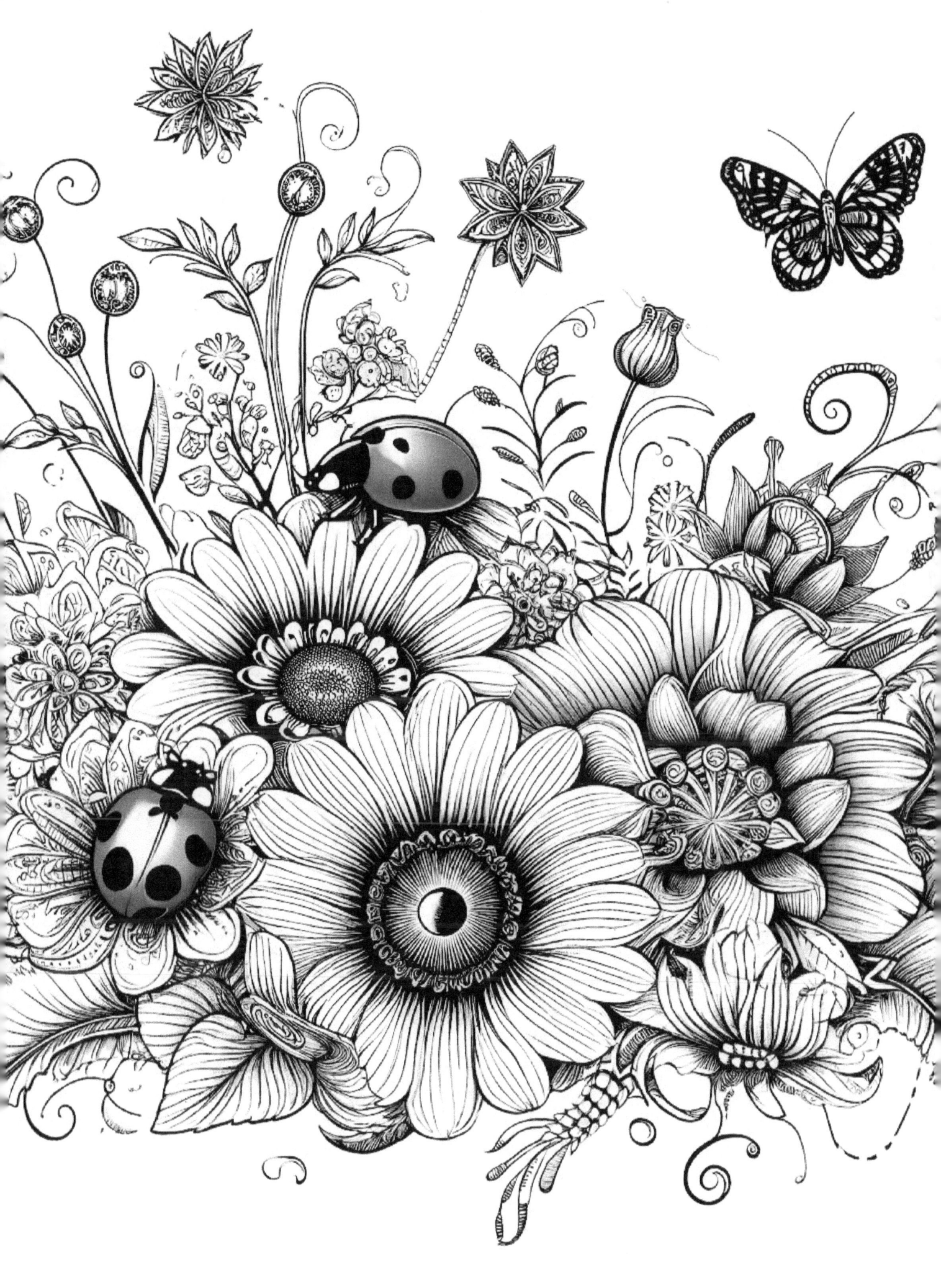

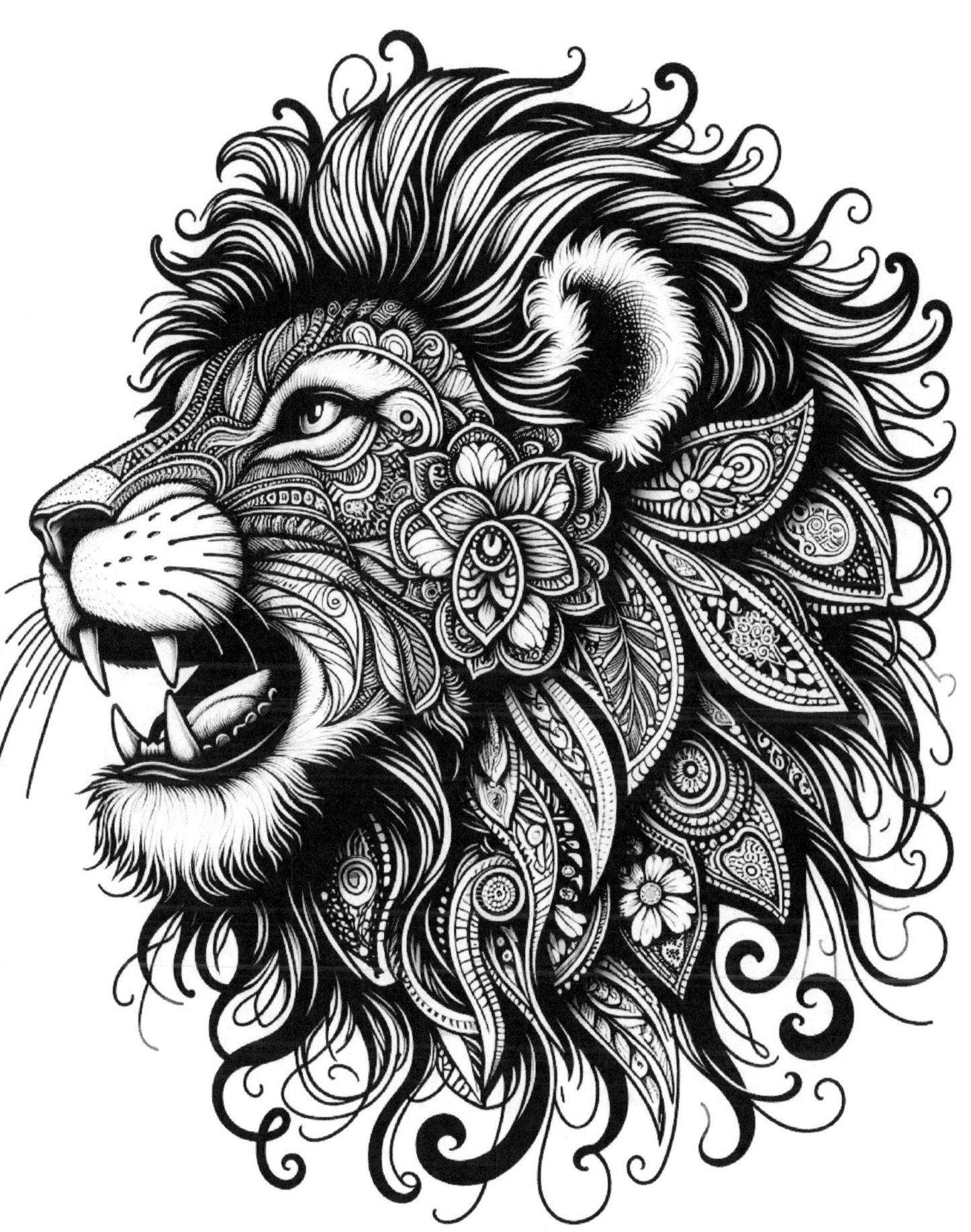

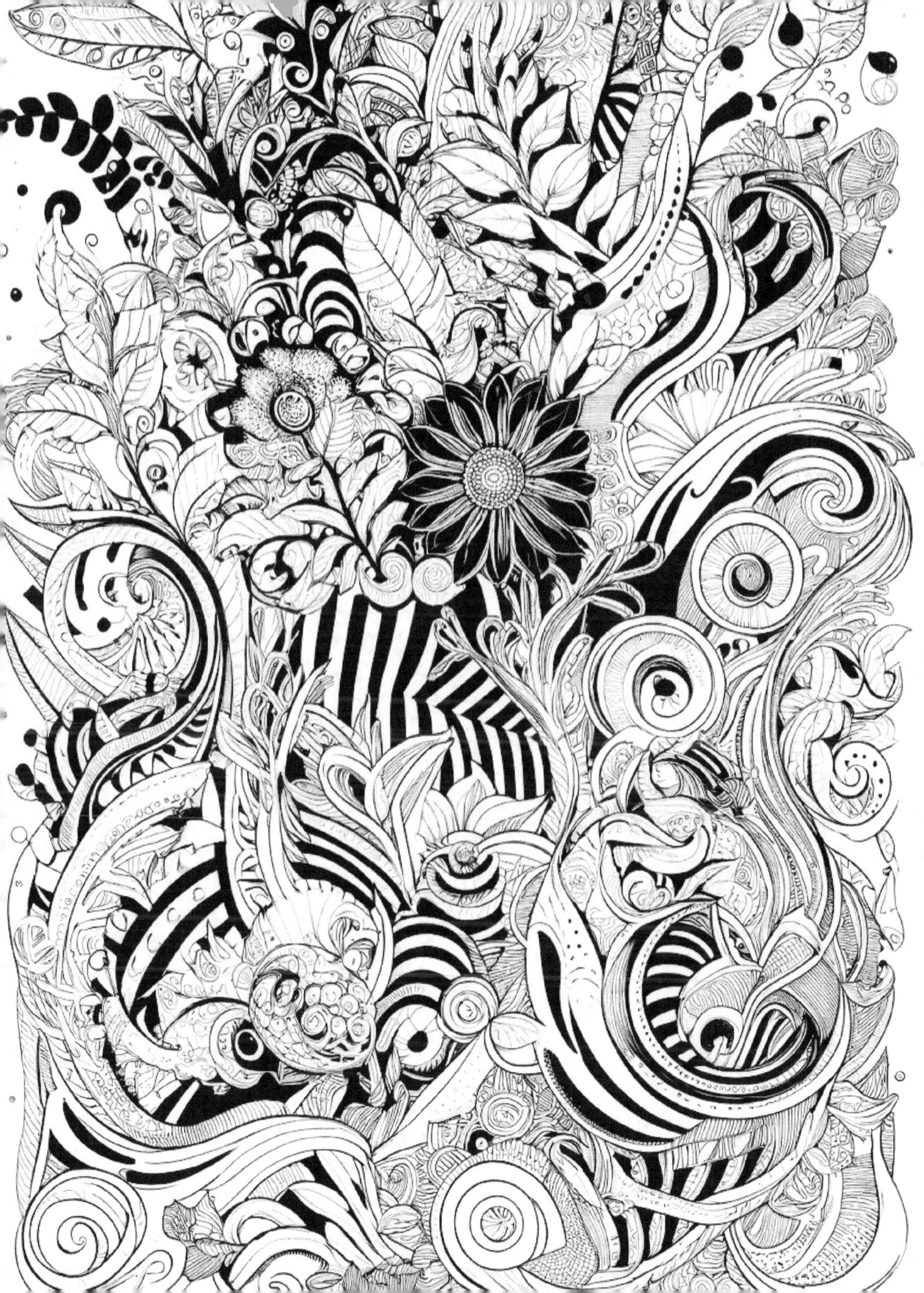

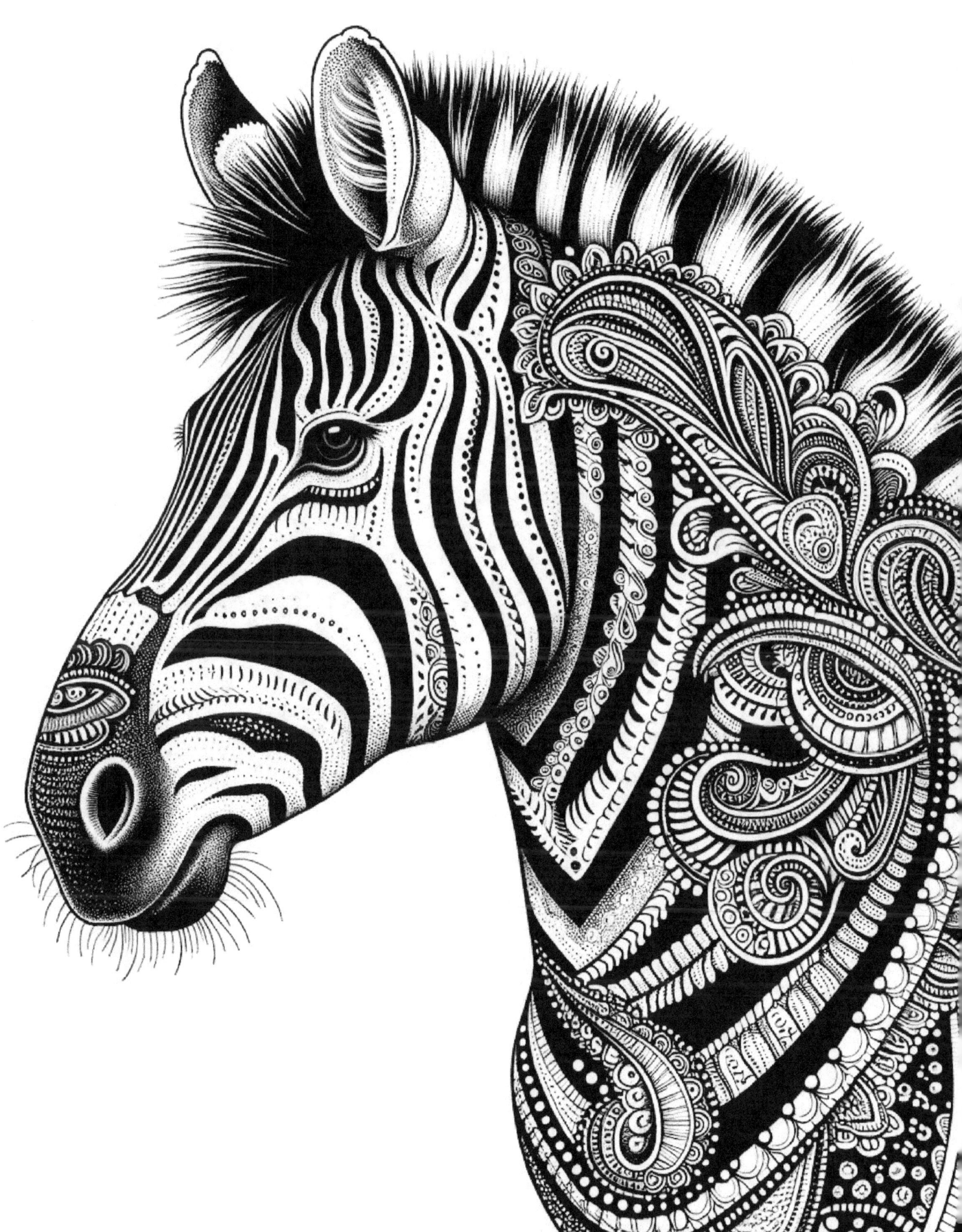

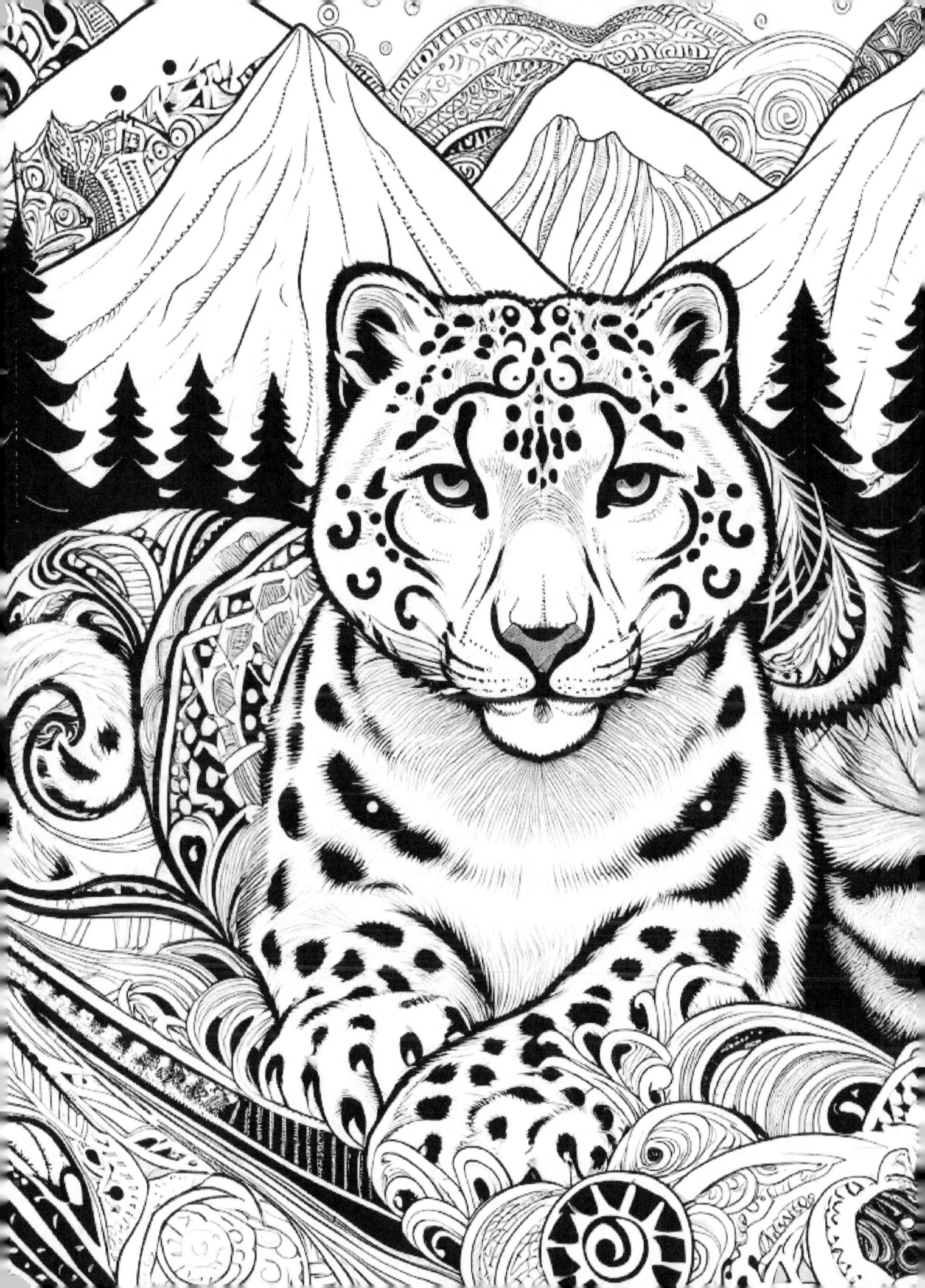

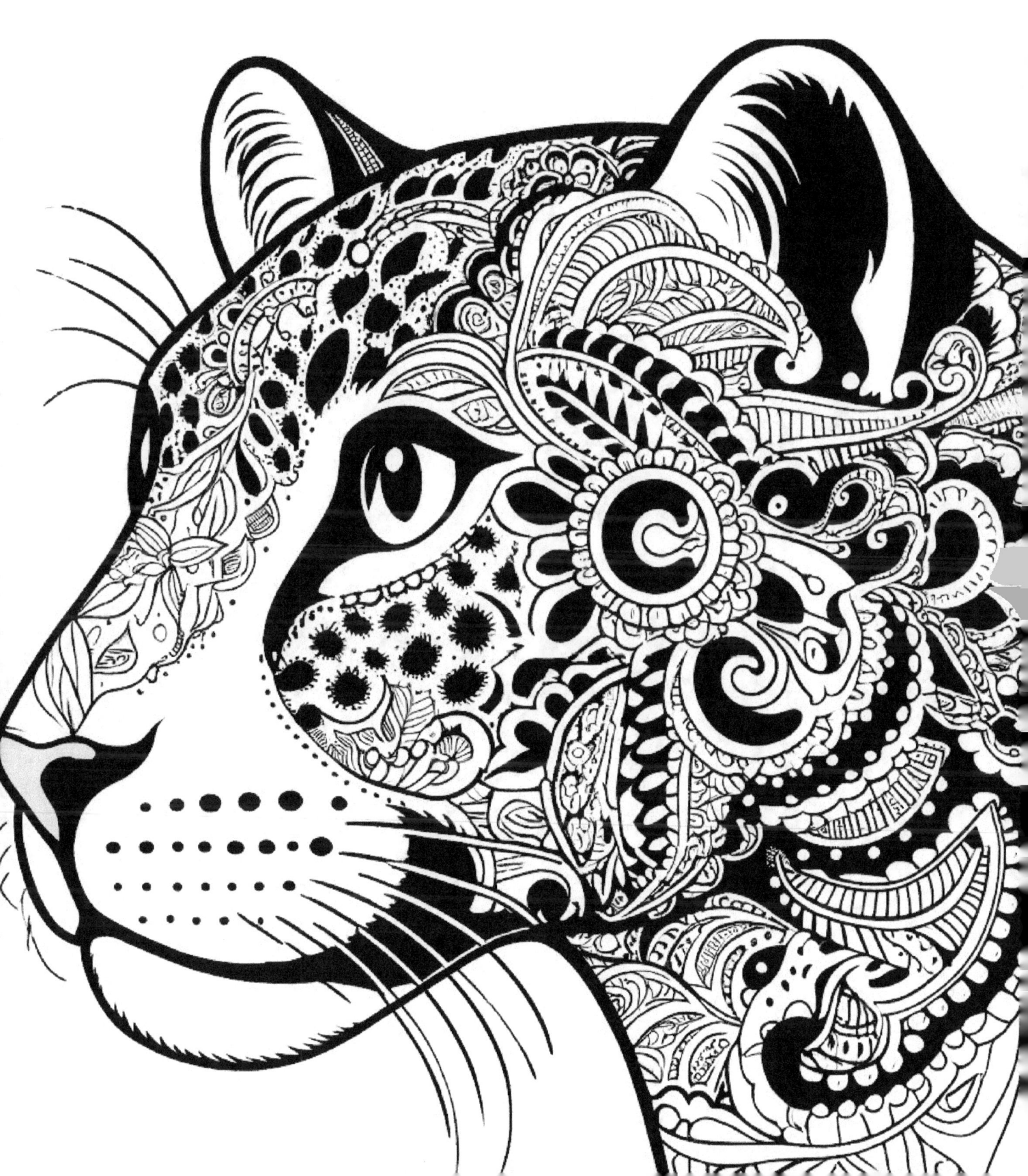

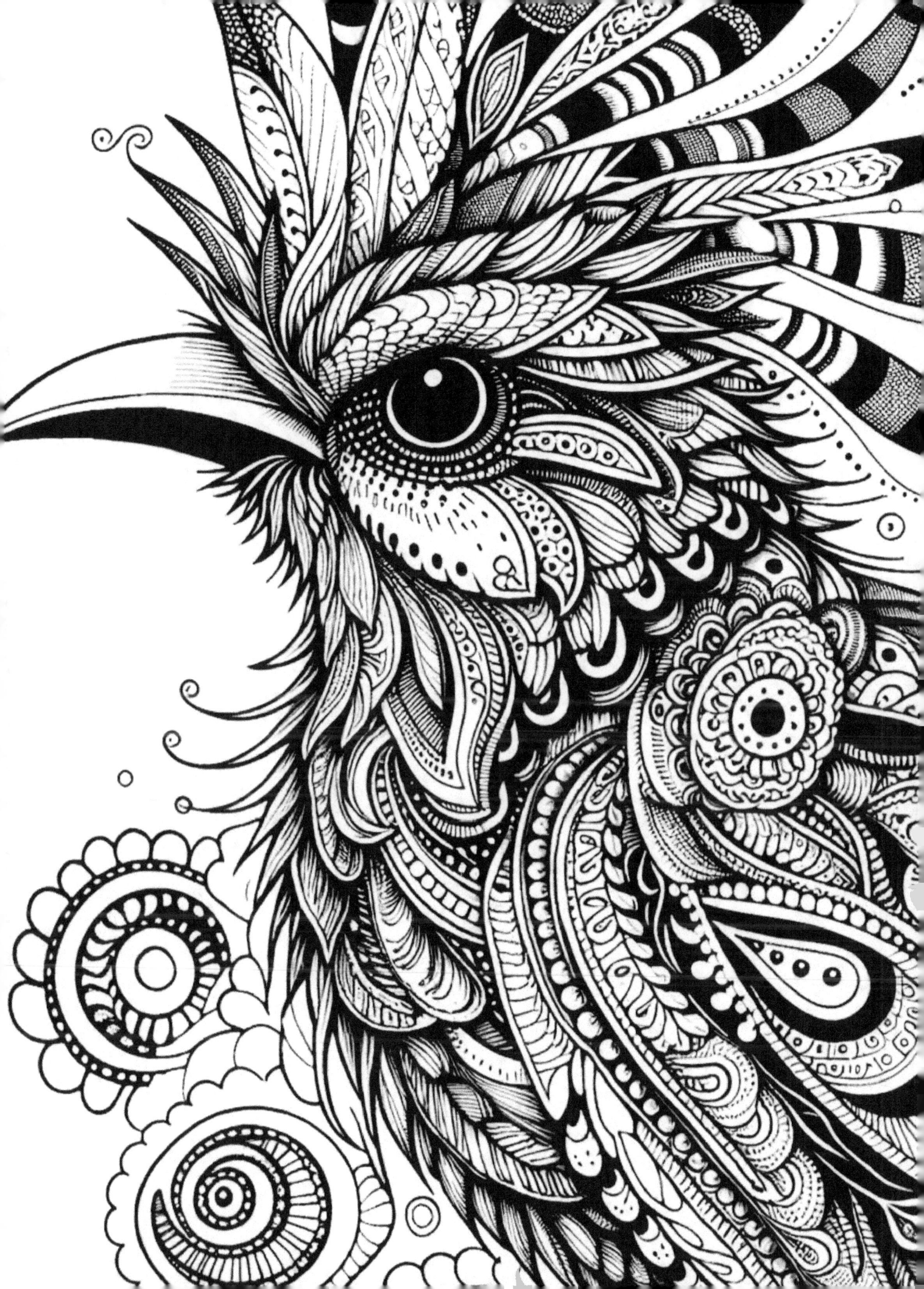

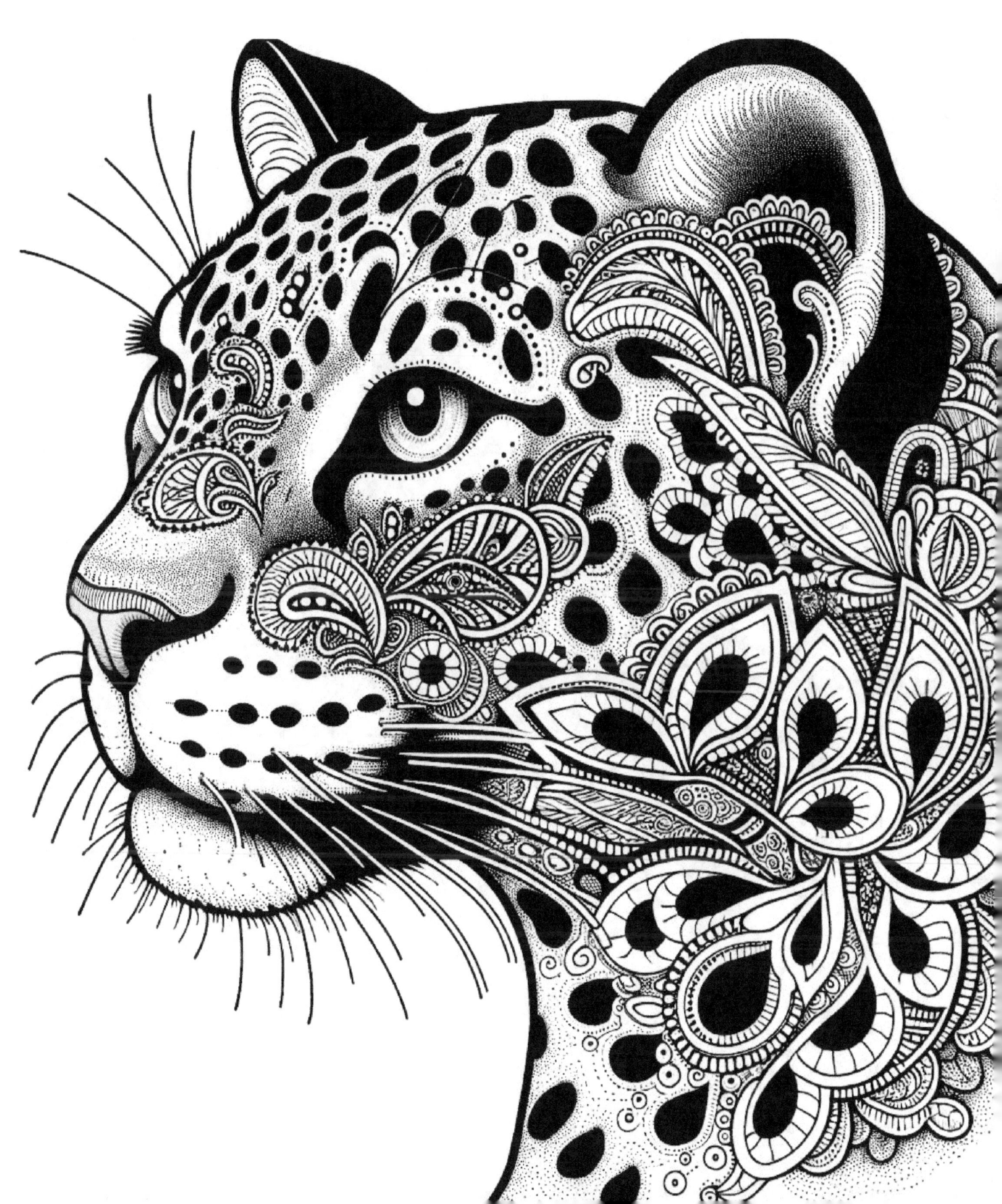

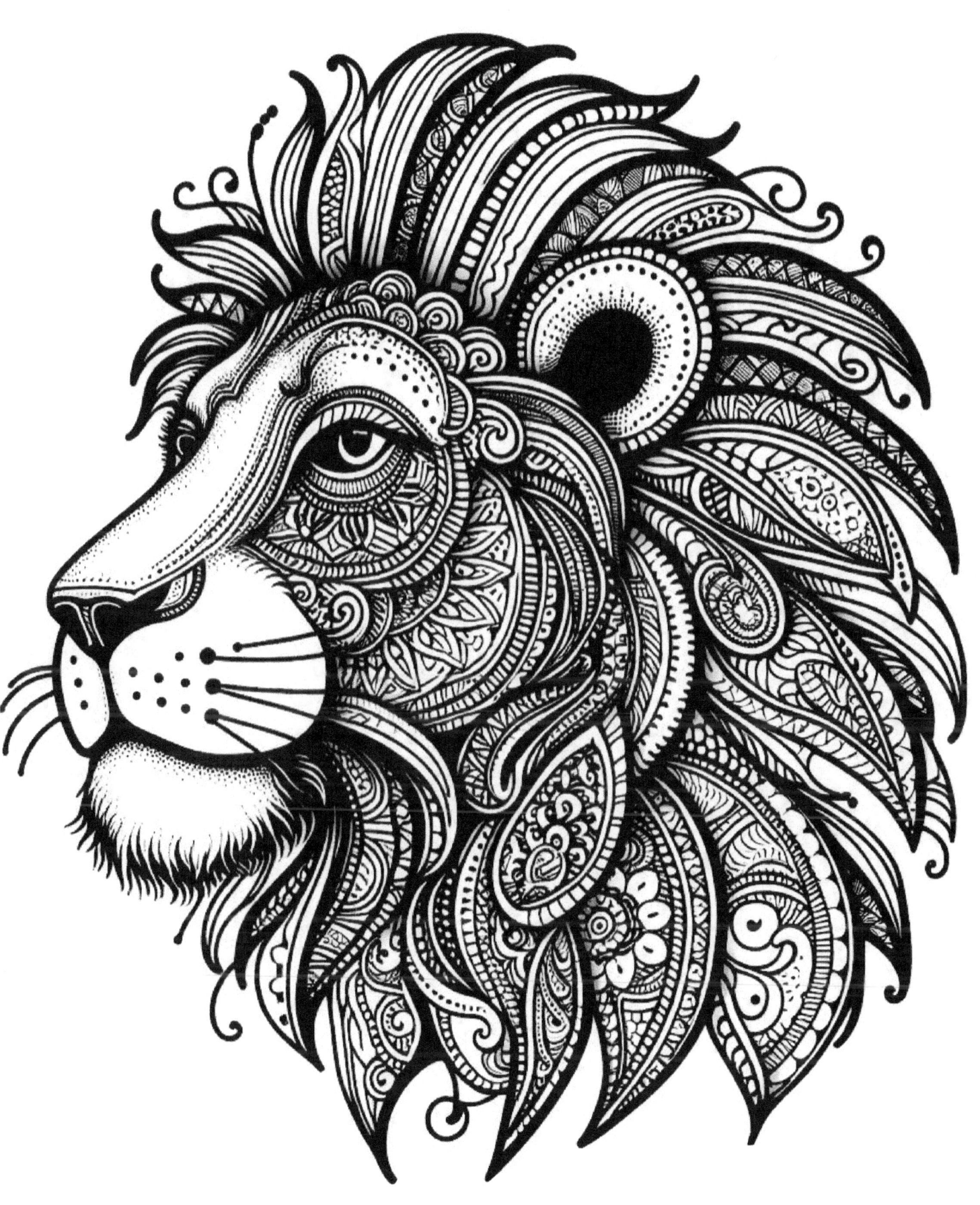

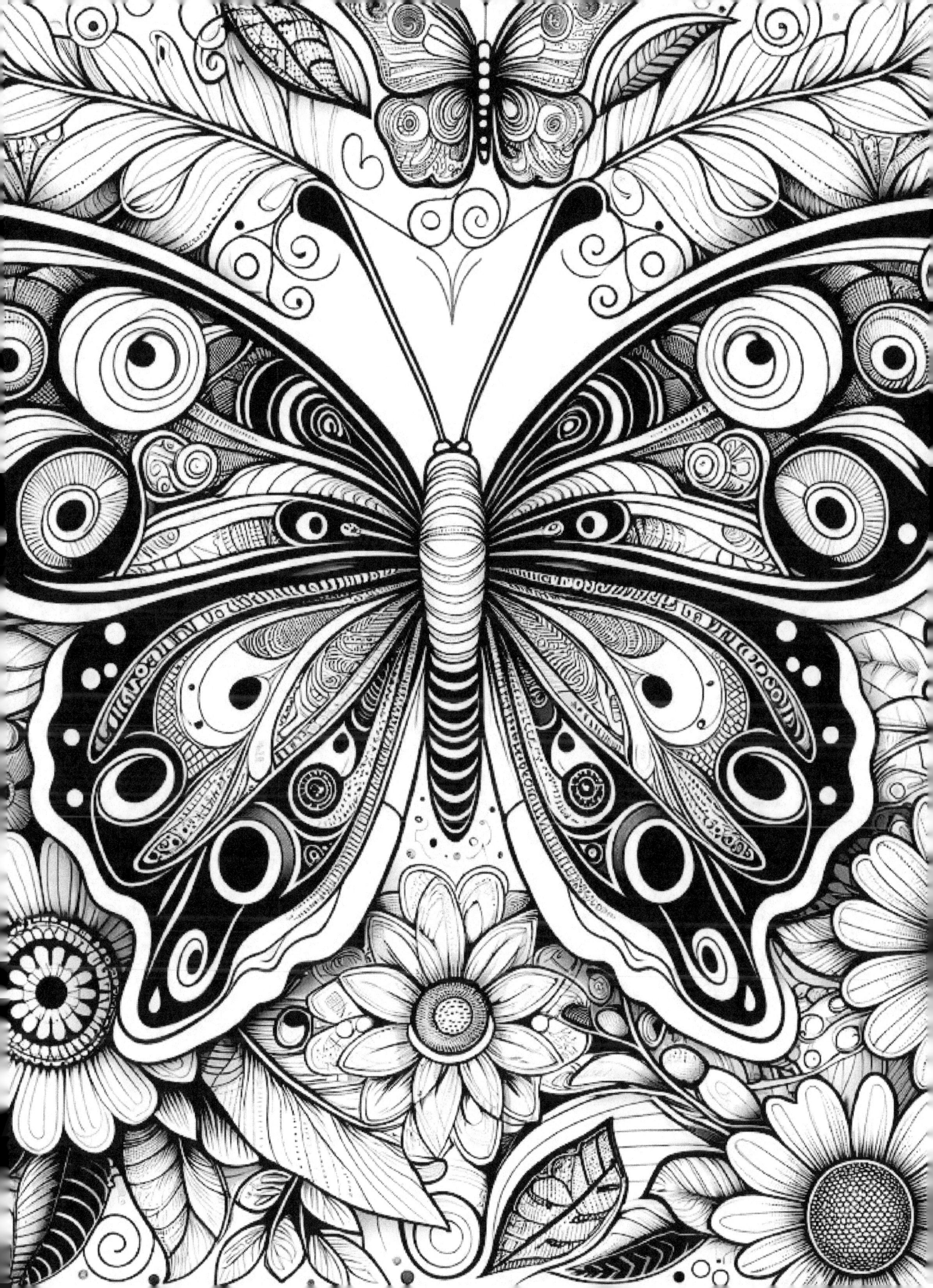

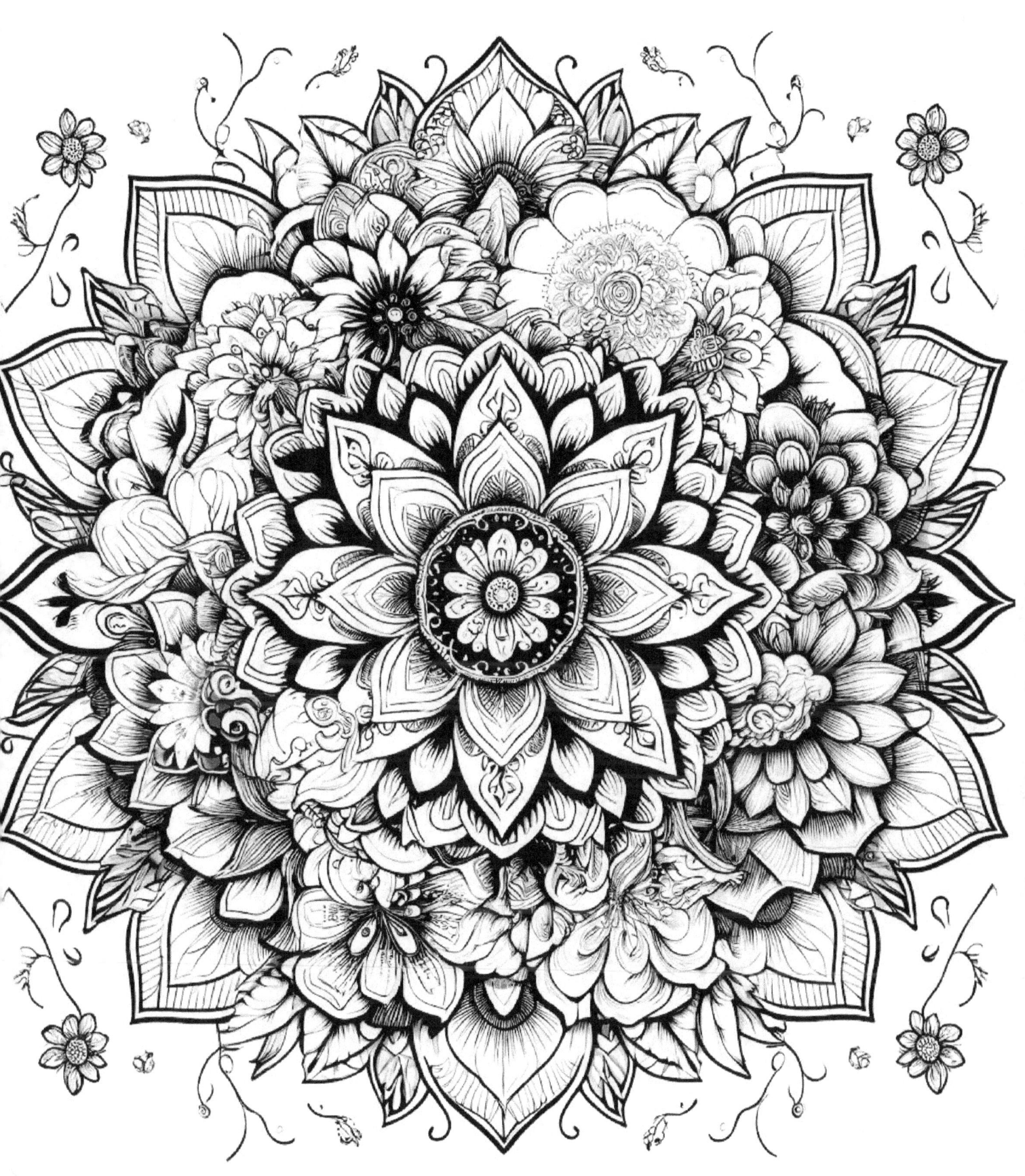

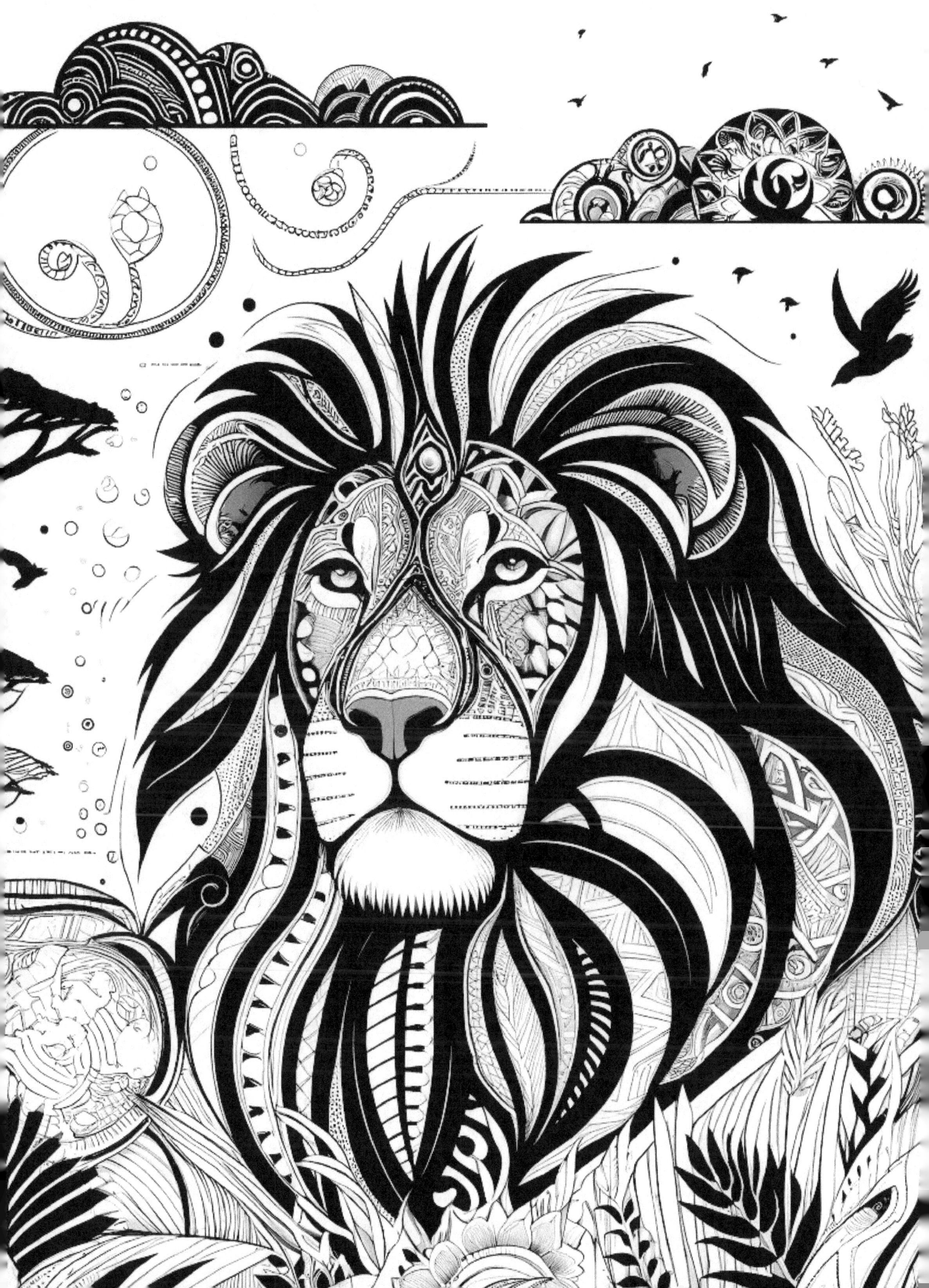

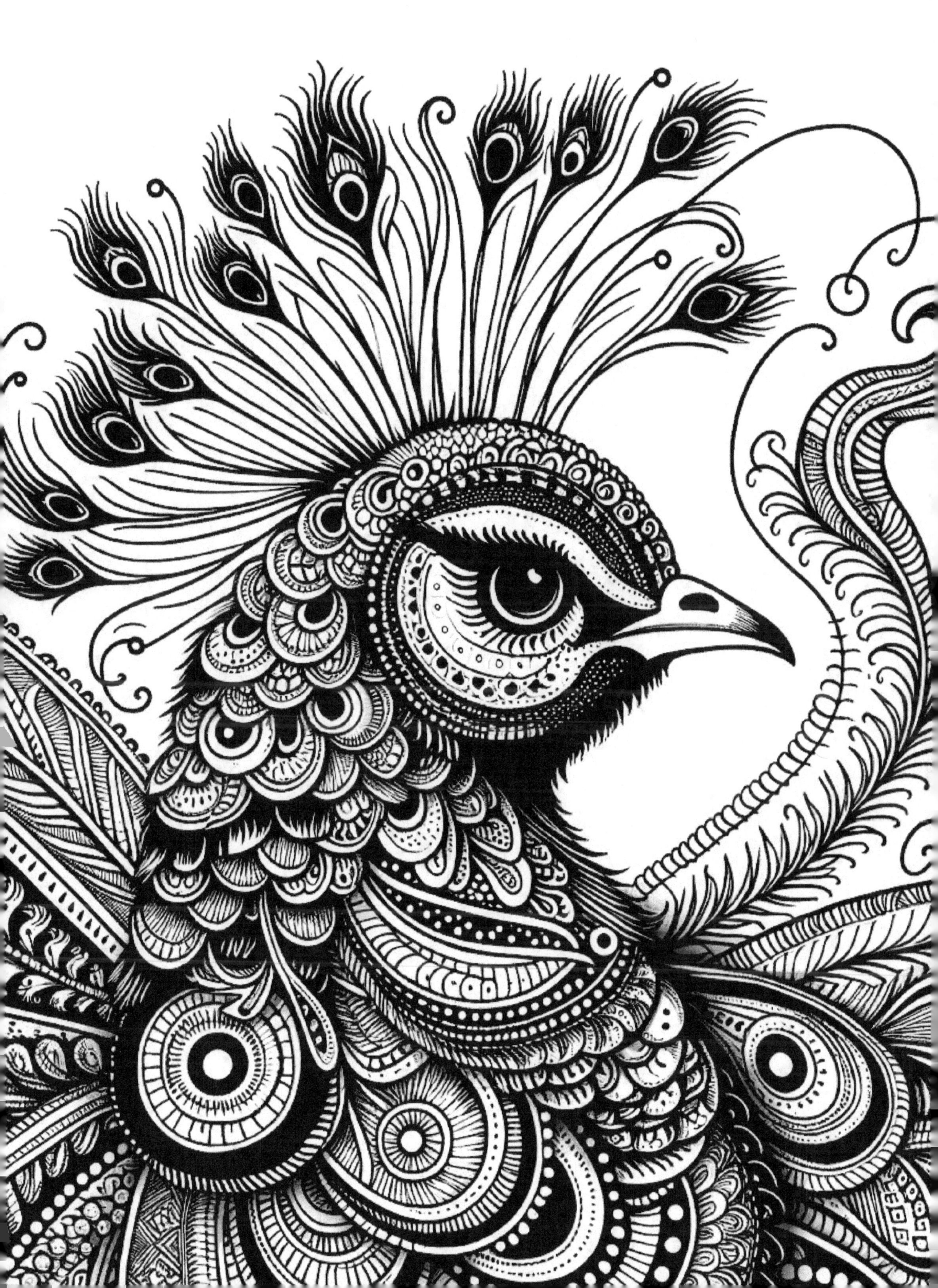

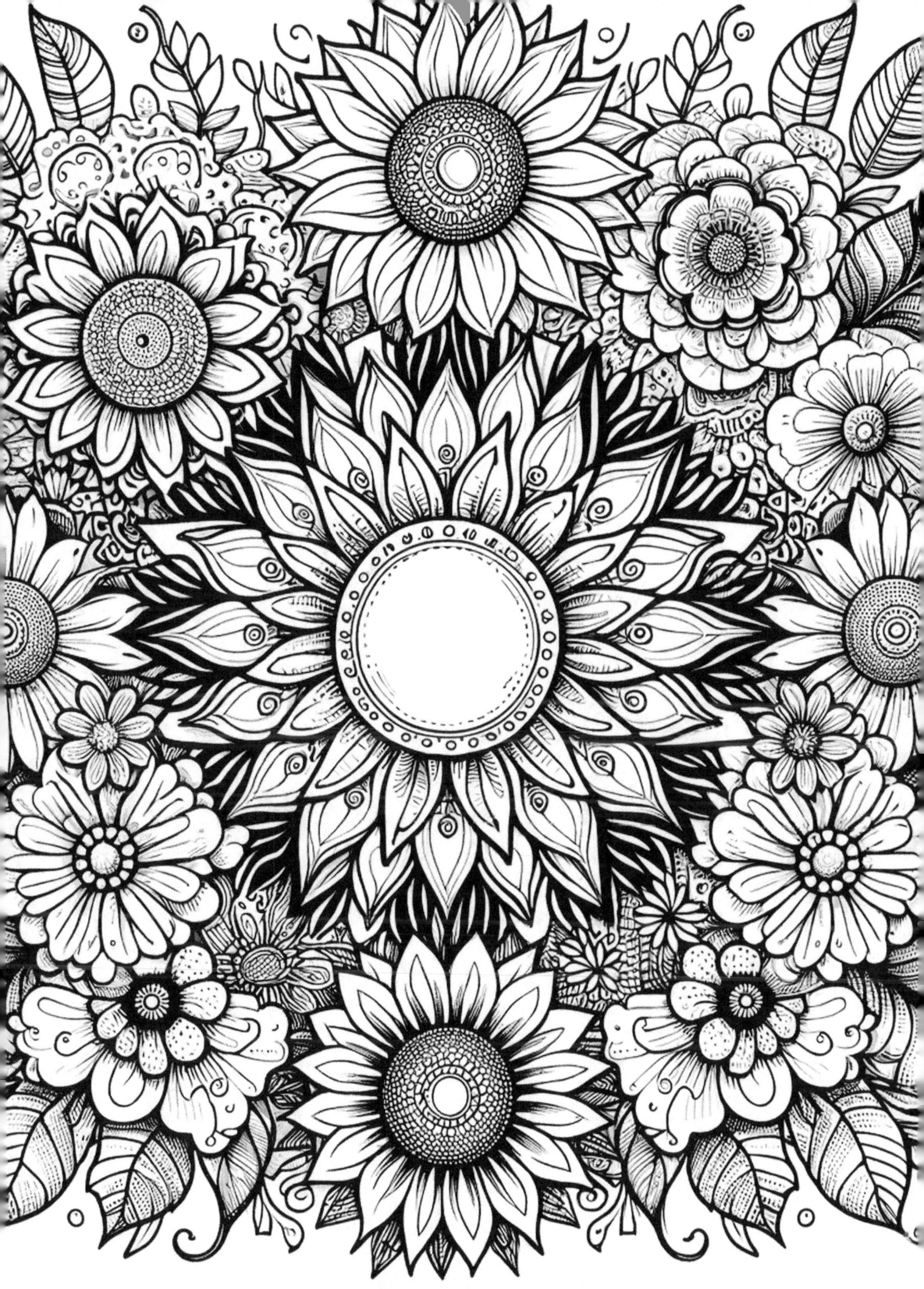

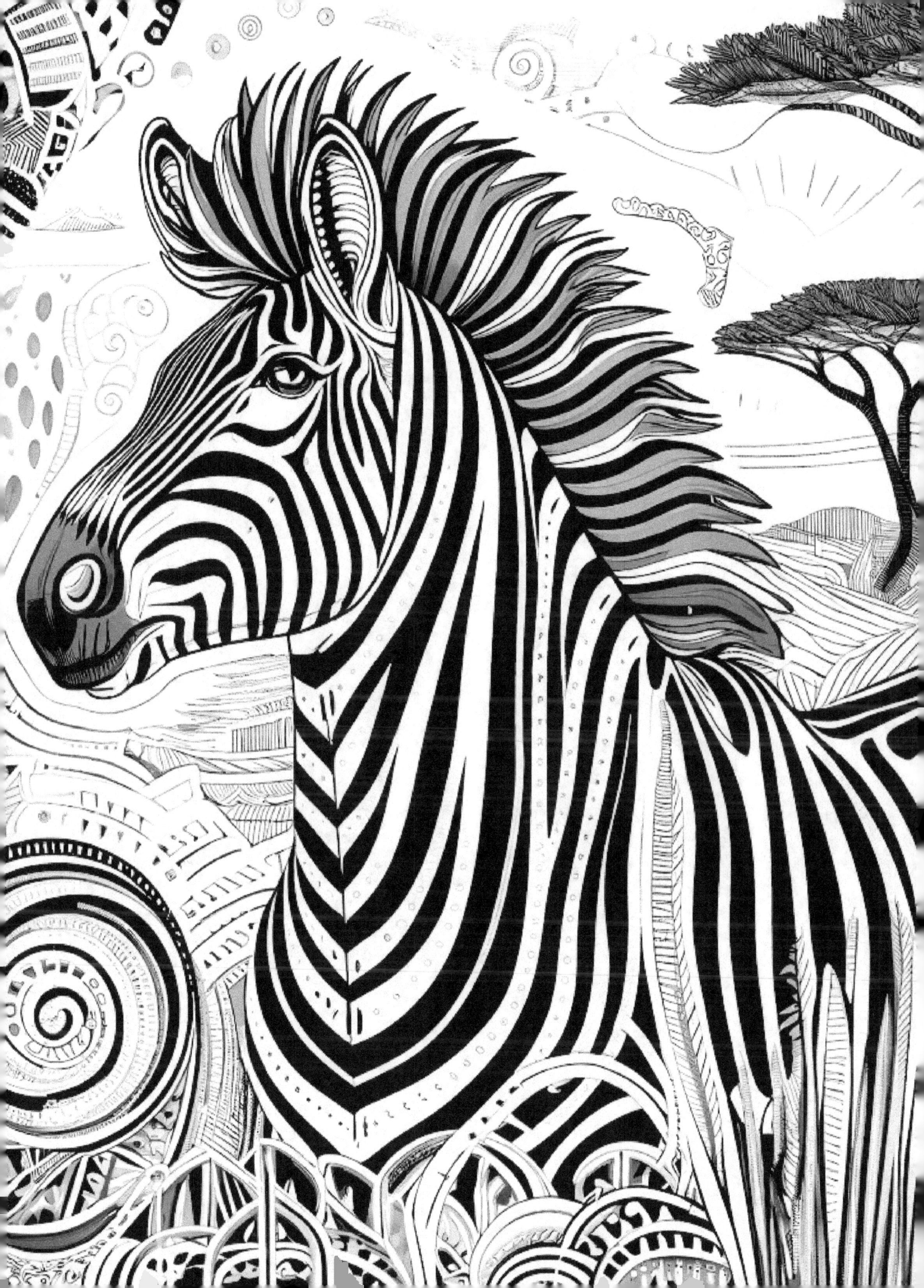

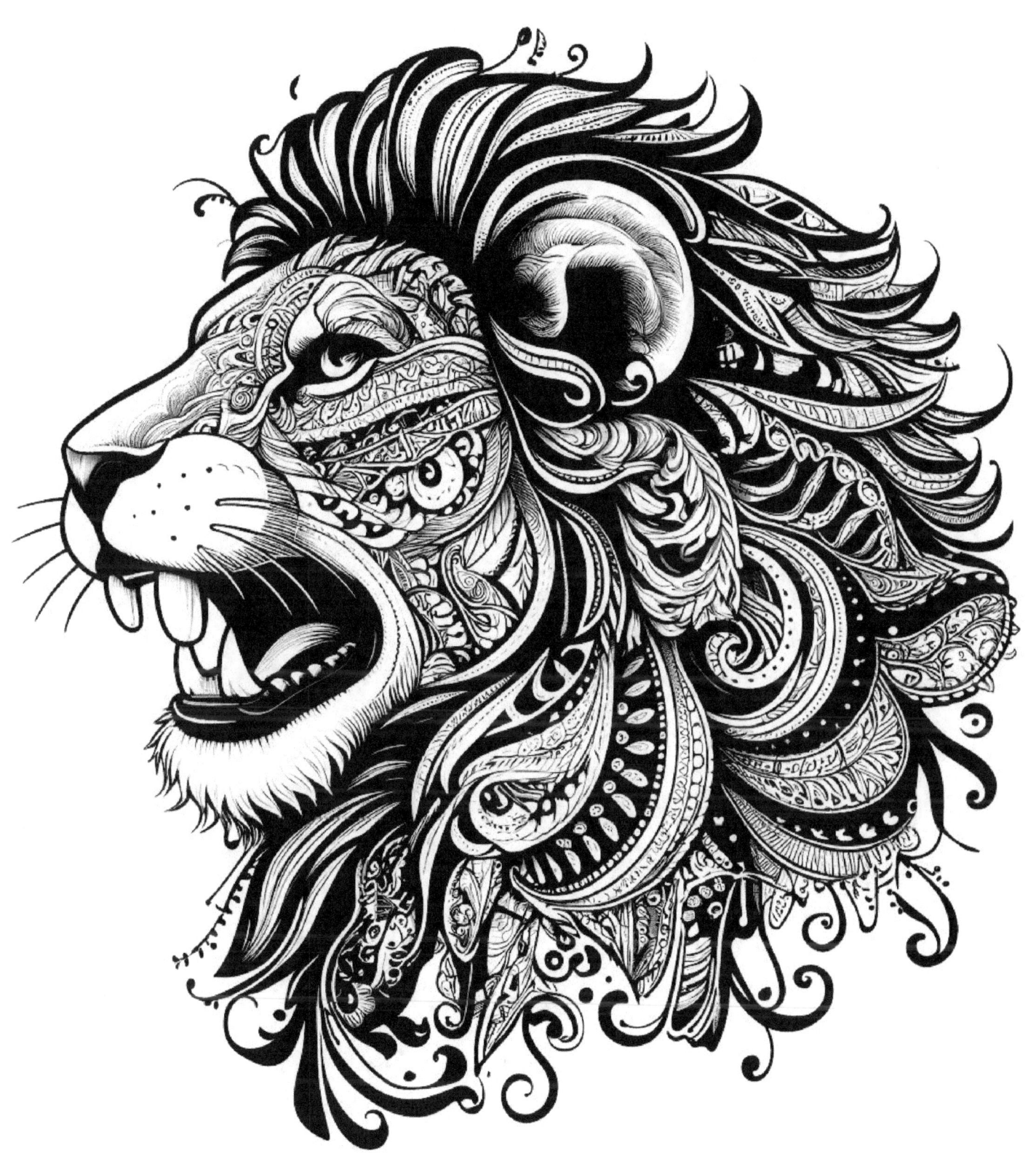

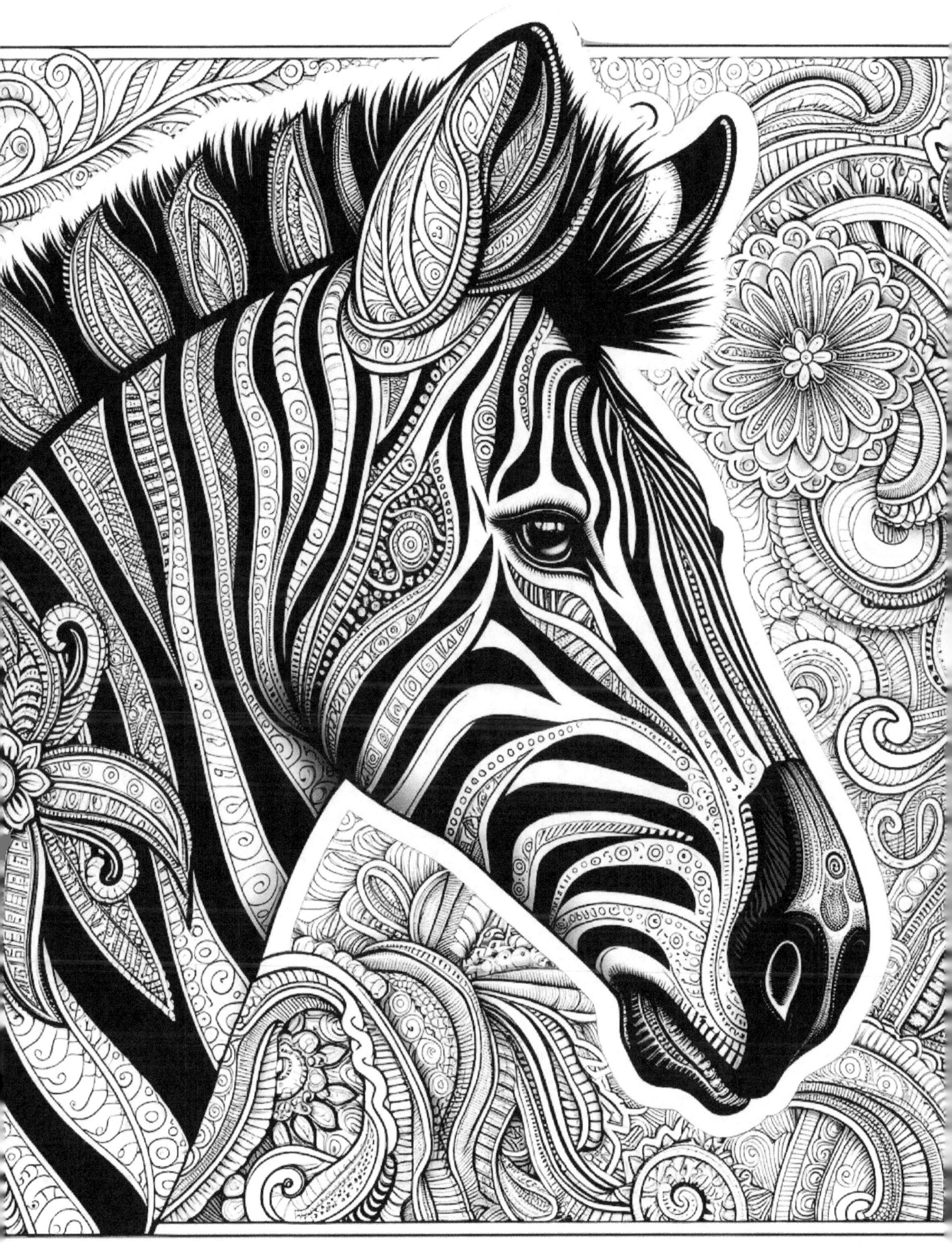

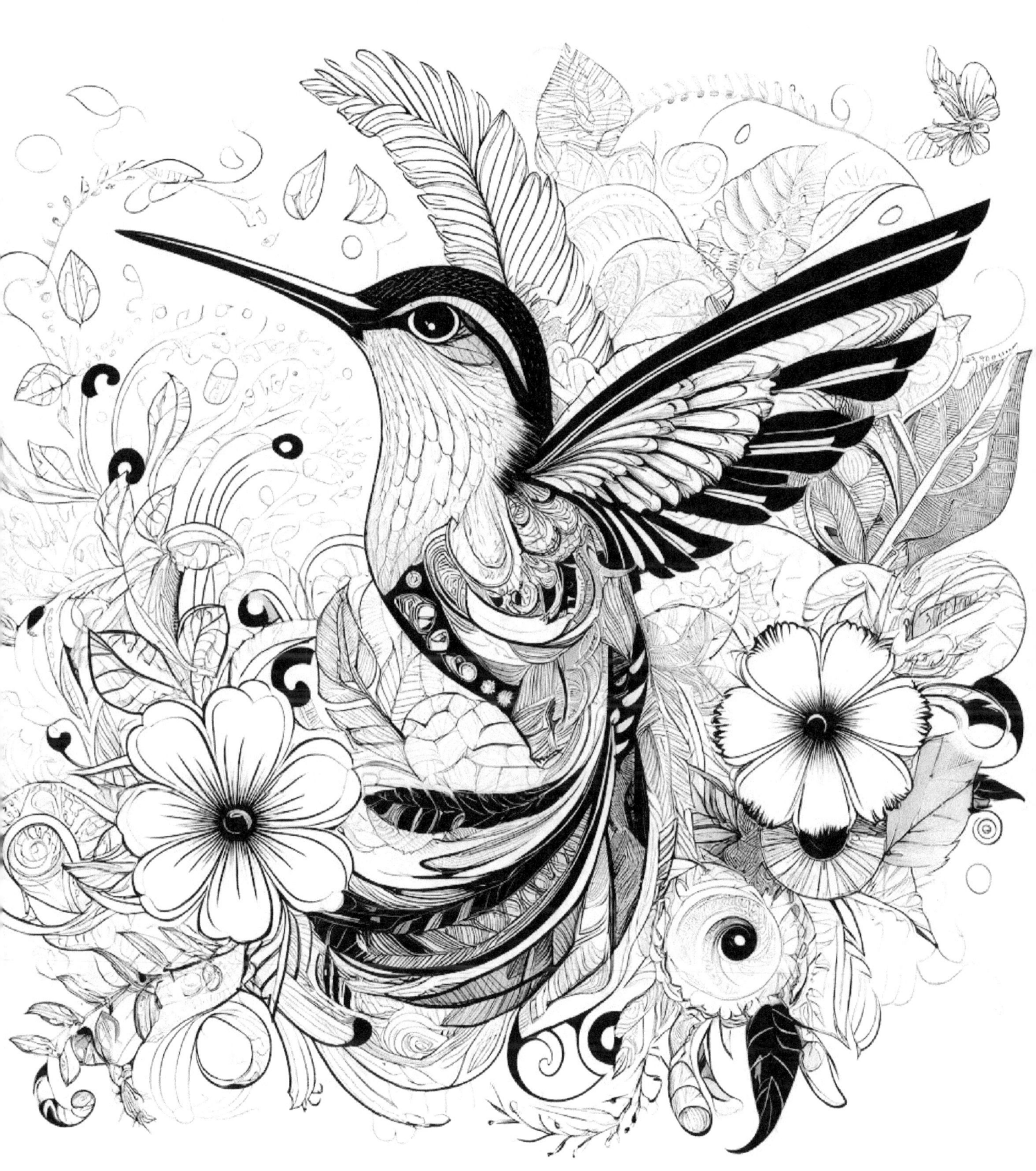

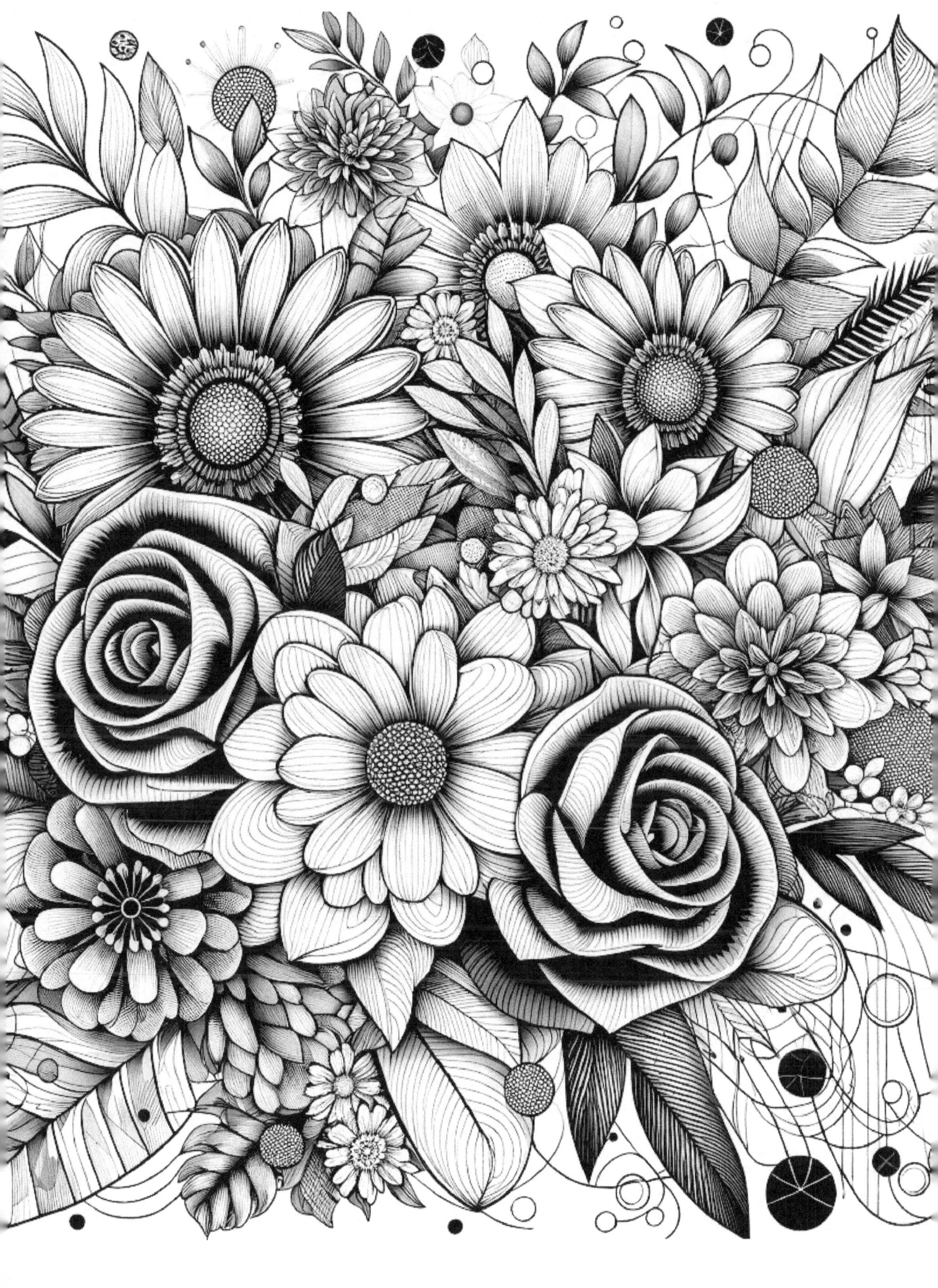

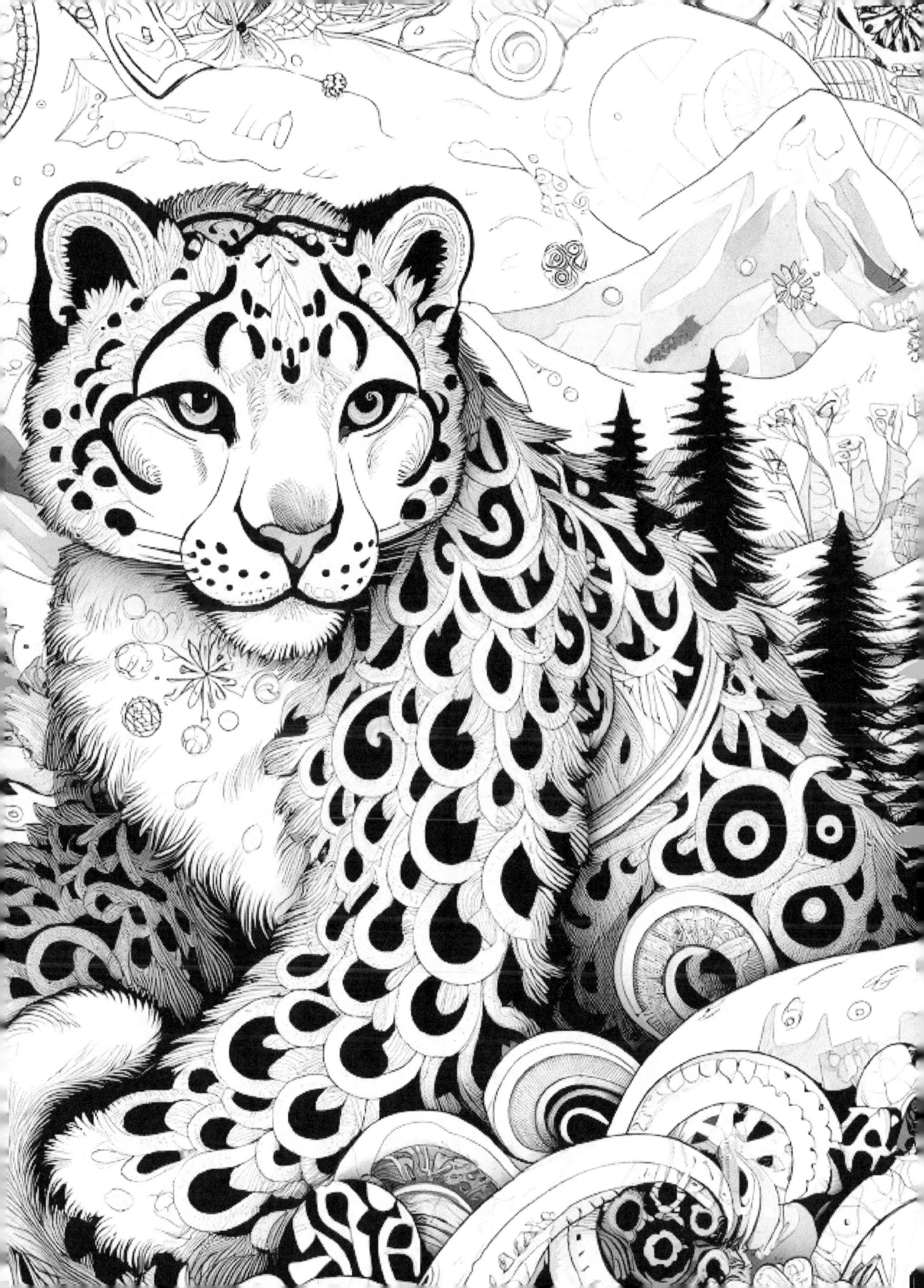

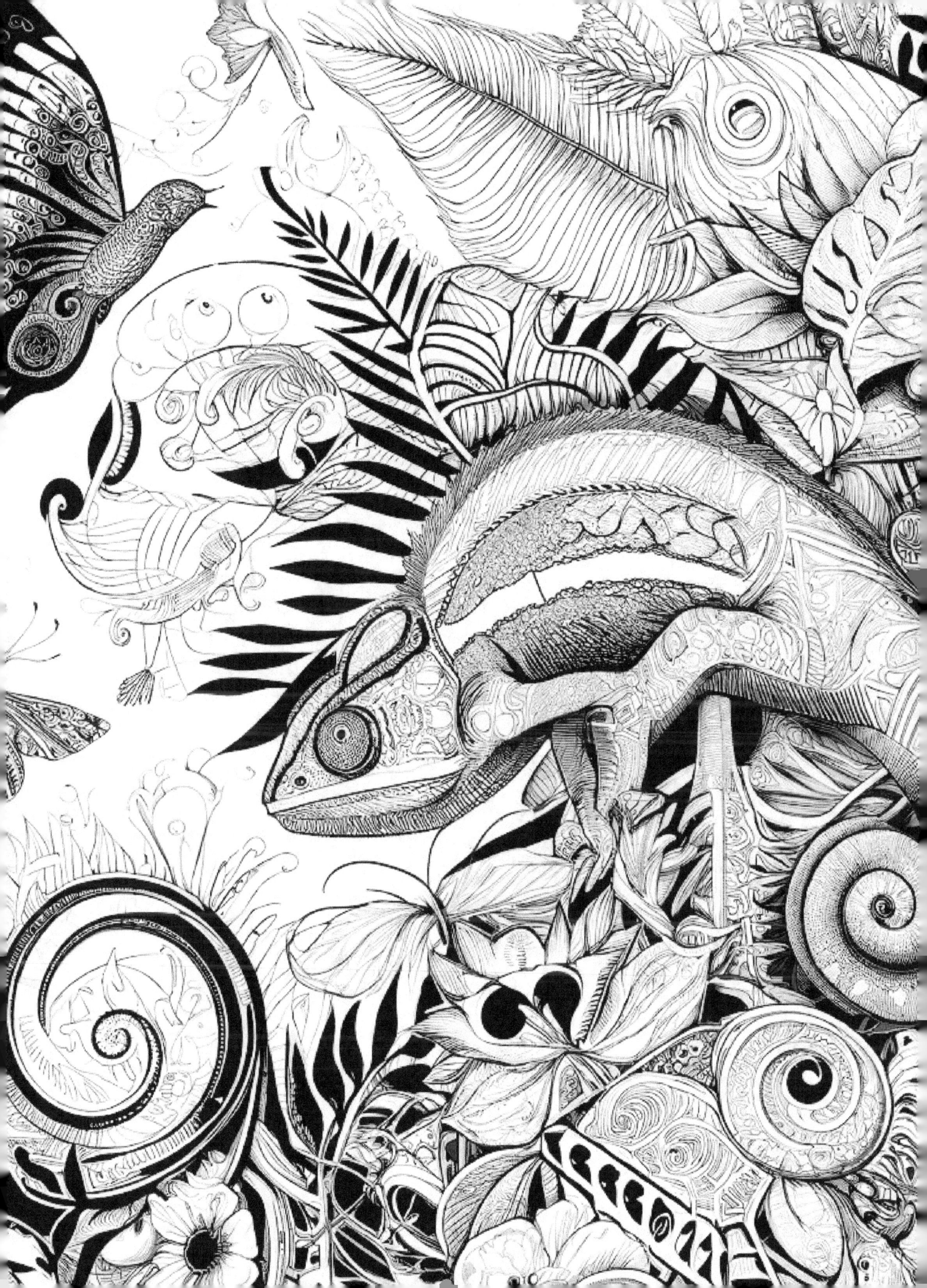

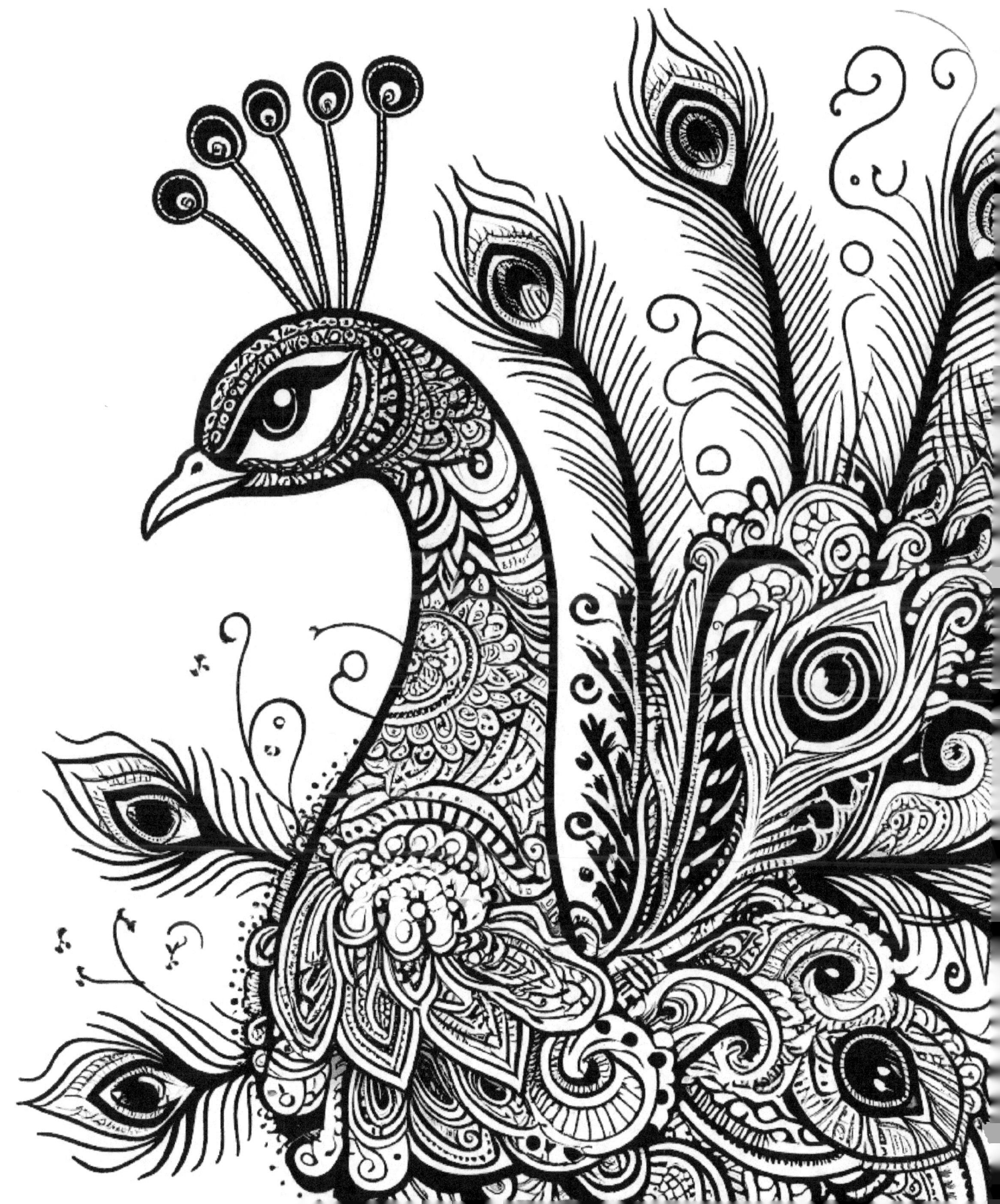

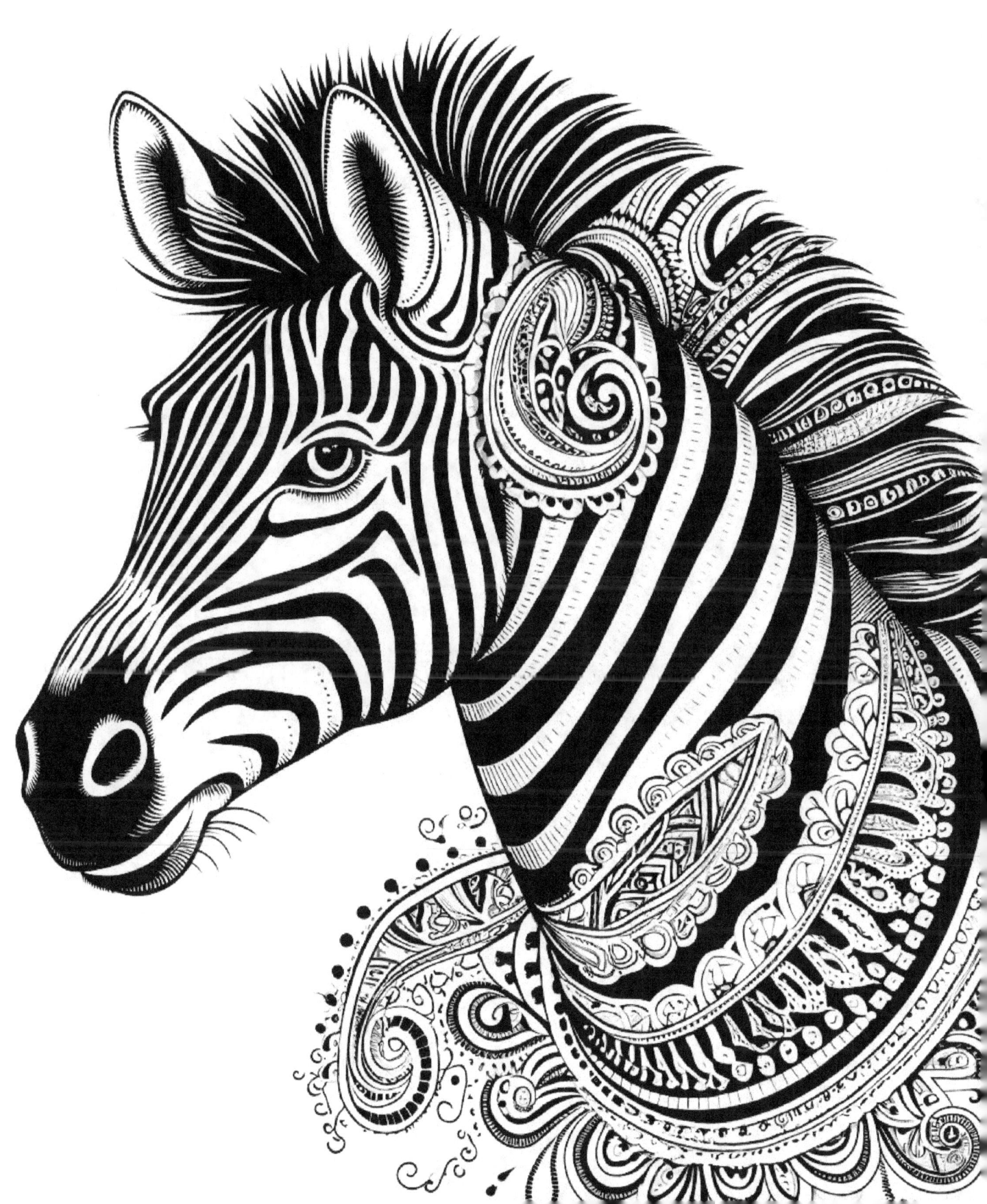

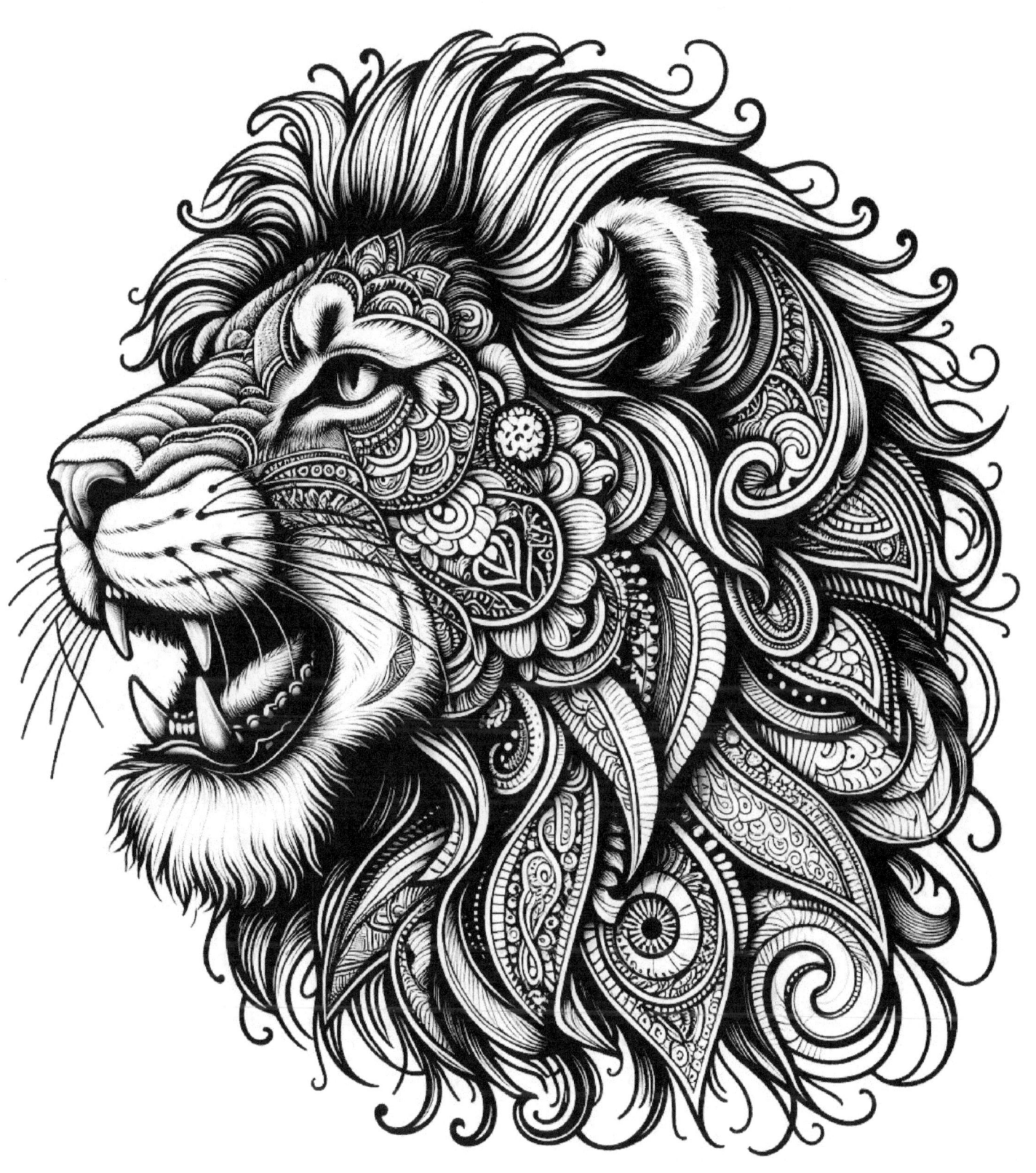

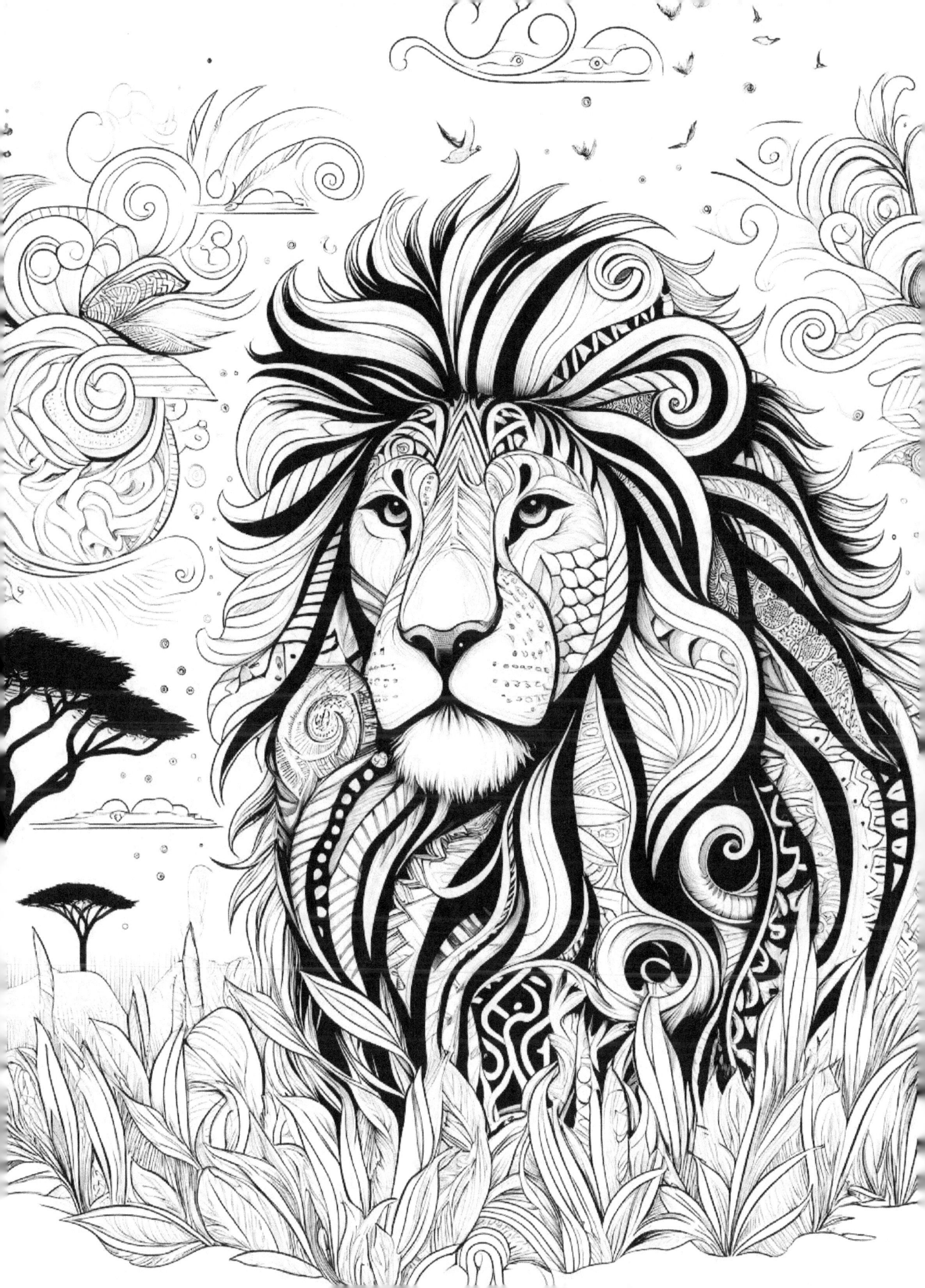

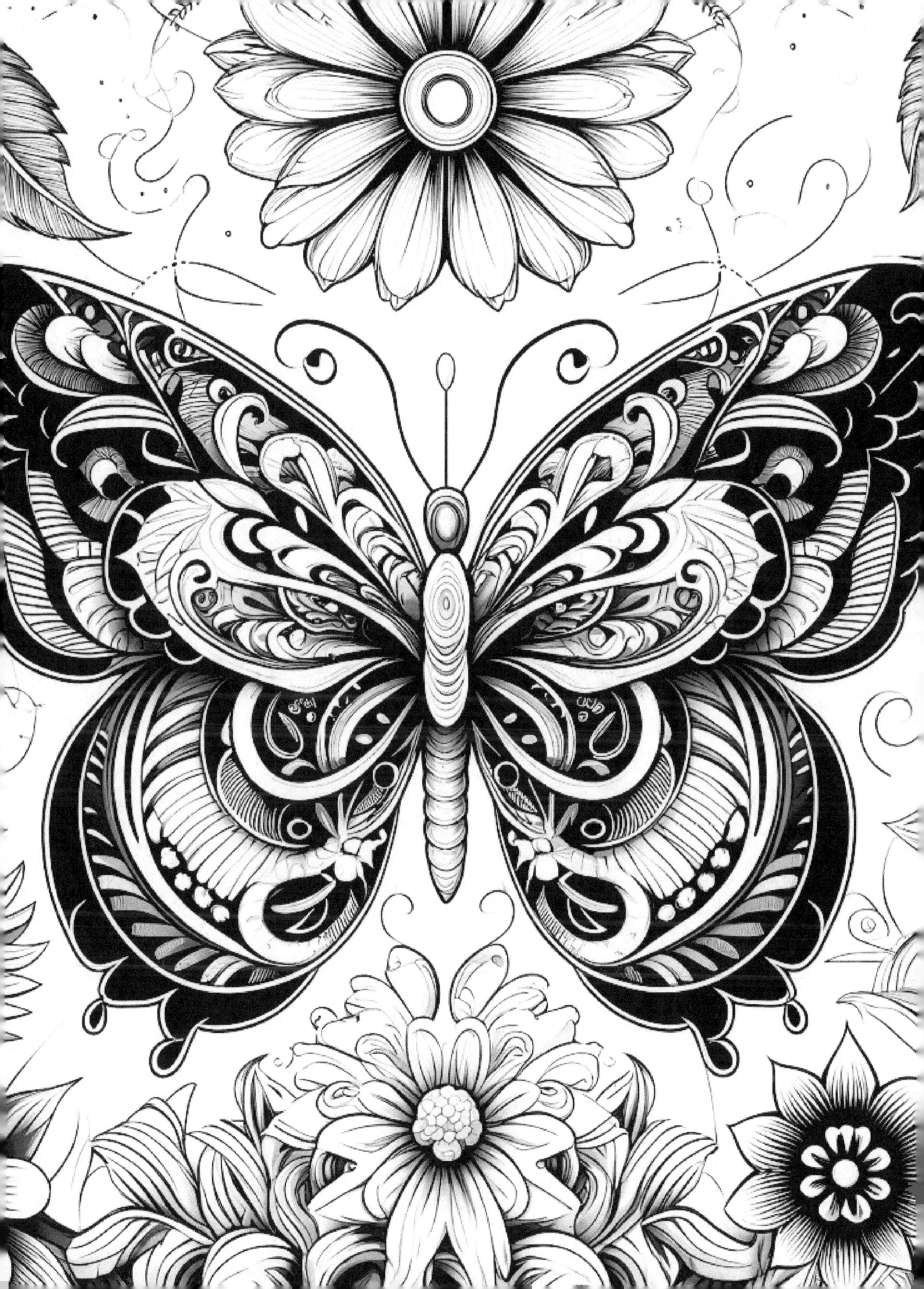

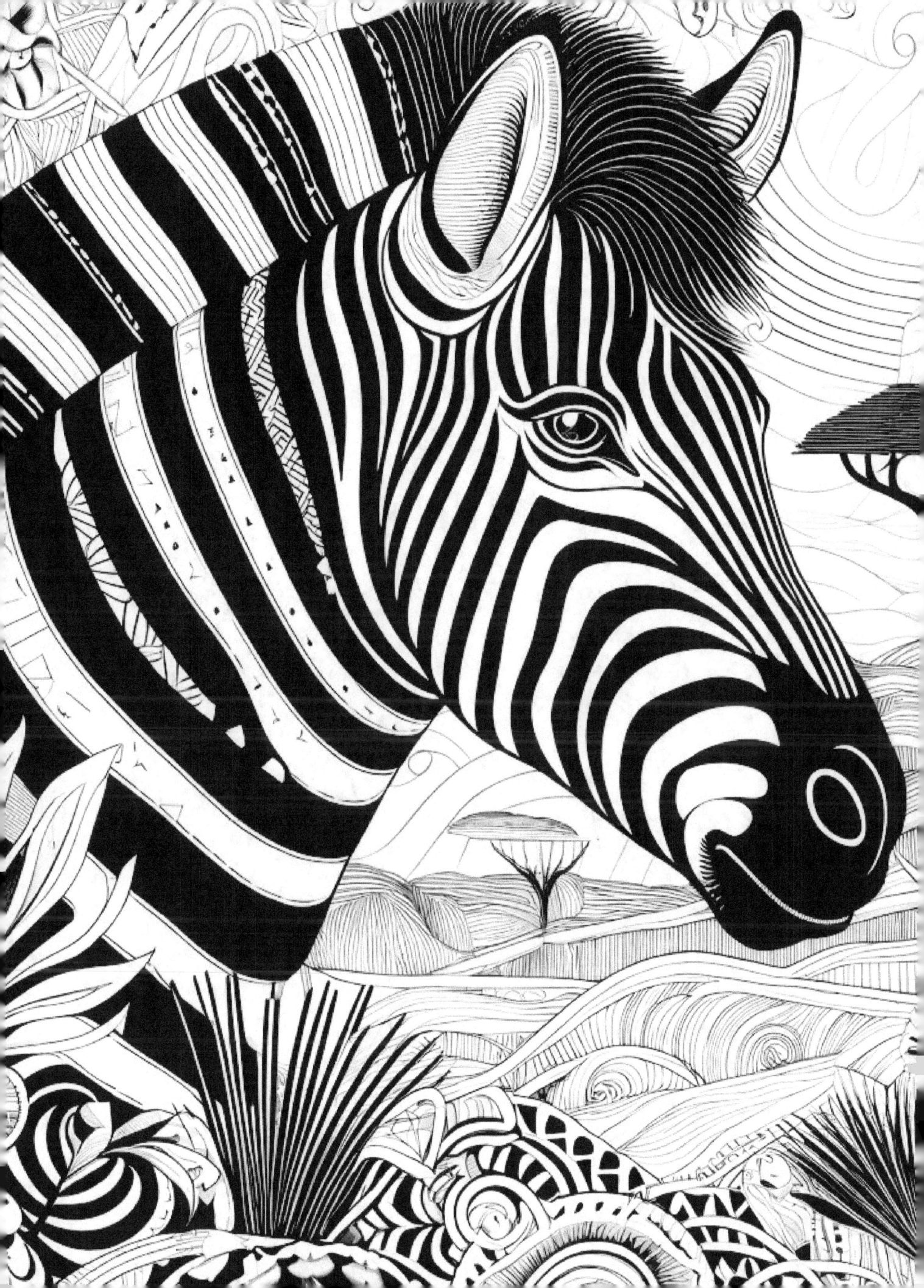

Thank you for joining us on this serene journey through nature. We hope "Nature's Serenity: Stress-Relieving Coloring Book for Adults" has provided you with moments of peace, creativity, and joy. As you have colored your way through these pages, we trust you have found a deeper connection to the beauty and tranquility that nature offers.

Remember, the process of coloring is not just about the finished artwork but also about the meditative experience of creating it. Keep this book handy for those times when you need a break from the hustle and bustle of everyday life, and let it serve as a reminder to slow down, breathe, and appreciate the simple pleasures around you.

We encourage you to continue exploring your creativity and finding joy in the little things. Until next time, may you always find serenity in nature and in your heart.